DENA
GLAZE

CURRIE

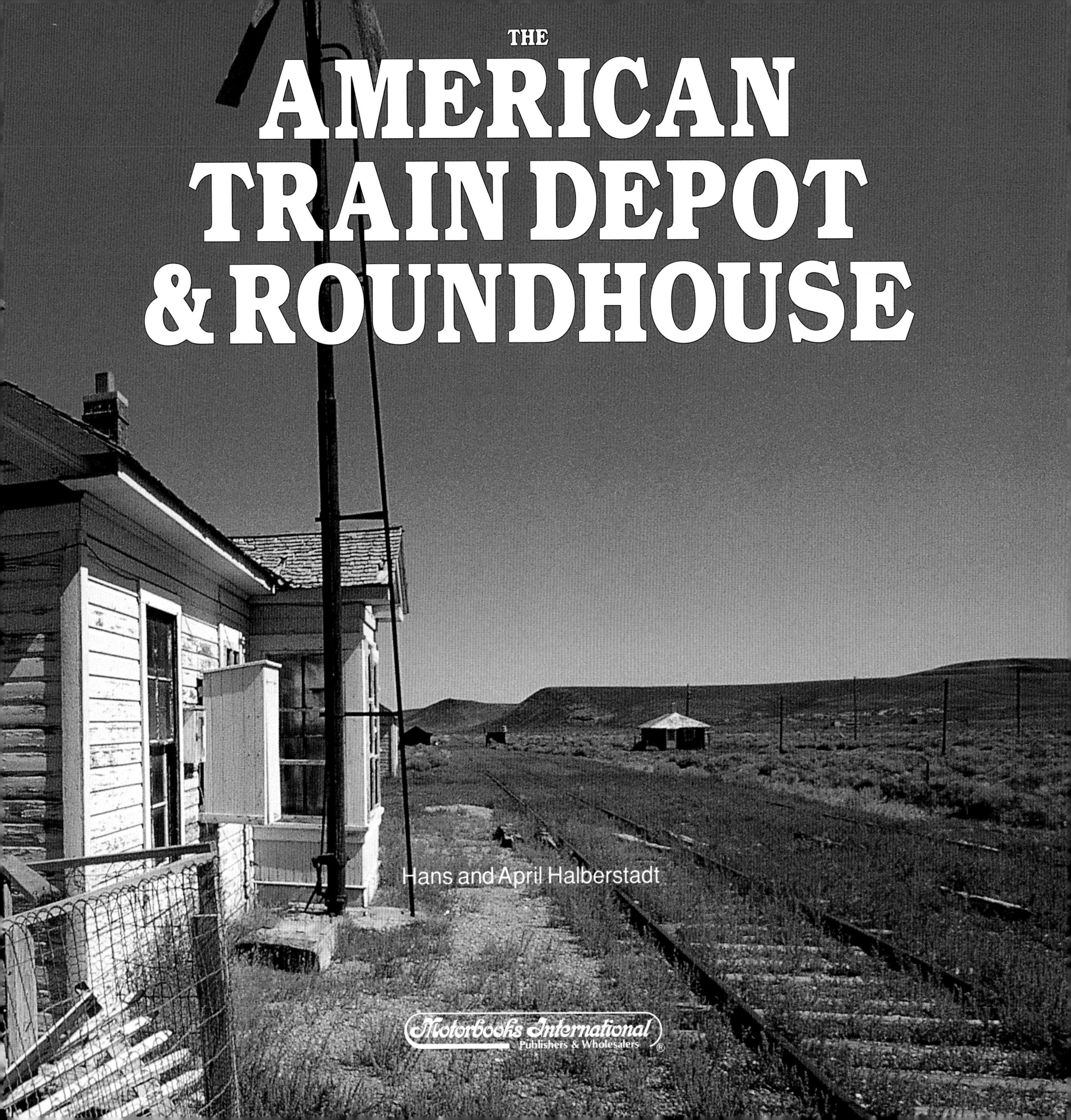

THE AMERICAN TRAIN DEPOT & ROUNDHOUSE

Hans and April Halberstadt

Motorbooks International
Publishers & Wholesalers

Dedication

To our parents:
John and Libby Hope
Hal and Olga Halberstadt

First published in 1995 by Motorbooks International Publishers & Wholesalers, PO Box 2, 729 Prospect Avenue, Osceola, WI 54020 USA

Library of Congress Cataloging-in-Publication Data
Halbertstadt, Hans.
The American train depot & roundhouse/ Hans M. and April Halberstadt.
p. cm.
Includes index.
ISBN 0-7603-0003-8
1. Railroad stations--United States. 2. Round houses (Railroads)--United States. I Title. II Title: American train depot and roundhouse.
TF302.U54H35 1995 94-46712
725' .33' 0973--dc20

On the front cover: The Menlo Park, California, depot still serves daily commuters running between points such as San Jose and San Francisco. It was built around 1865 and was long a hub for Stanford University students at the start and end of the school year.

On the frontispiece: Traditional red and weathered in the Nevada sun, this service barn is one of the Nevada Northern buildings near Ely, Nevada.

On the title page: Currie, Nevada, is small and remote, but even it had a depot to serve passengers. The depot was primarily a crew change facility, but passengers could board here as well.

On the acknowledgments page: Elbow grease and big wheels such as those on this luggage cart would help move a family's luggage across the platform from their coach or taxi to the train.

On the back cover: No. 28 heads out of the Sierra RR roundhouse at Jamestown, California, for another day of tourist excursion rides. *Mike Halberstadt* The bay window facing the tracks gave the agent at the Sioux Falls, South Dakota, depot a good view of the tracks and trains. *Hans Halberstadt* Telegraph wires run to the quaint Woodridge depot, whose walls bear some early forms of outdoor advertising for products such as cleanser and crackers. *Library of Congress*

Printed in Hong Kong

Contents

Acknowledgments

A multitude of people care for and about America's railroad resource, and we've met a lot of them while working on this book. It is a friendly, generous, visionary crowd—lucky for us. Some of the folks who contributed are listed below, and we are indebted to them. In addition, another multitude of folks along the right-of-way, sometimes anonymously, pointed us in interesting directions. Thanks to all.

Tom Anderson; historian, Grand Island, Nebraska
Bob Auman; Public Relations, Norfolk Southern railway
Linda Bailey; Cincinnati Museum, Cincinnati, Ohio
Jim Bartz; author and railroad historian
Henry Bender, Jr.; California Railroad Historian, San Jose, California
Fred Bennett; San Jose Historical Museum, San Jose, California
Mary Canchola; Santa Clara, California
Dr. Robert Chandler; Wells Fargo History Room, San Francisco, California
Beverly Fleming; State Historic Preservation Office, Independence, Missouri
Mike Green; South San Francisco, California
Kathleen Halcro; Independence, Missouri
John F. Hope, Esq.; Kansas City, Missouri
Maeve Hope Horton; St. Louis, Missouri
David Koenig; New Jersey Transit
Glory Ann Laffey; San Jose, California
Jim Leany; Grand Junction, Colorado
George Lund; AIA, Kansas City Union Station, Kansas City, Missouri
Sharon Mahoney; Amtrak, Washington, D.C.
Henry Marnette; Raytown, Missouri
Dick Mauer; Southern Pacific, ret., Santa Clara, California
Connie Menninger; Topeka, Kansas
L. L. Nieman
Harriet Parcells; National Association of Railway Passengers, Washington, DC
Ed Peterman; South Bay Historical Railroad Society
Sean Pitts; Nevada Northern Railway, East Ely, Nevada
Max Purdy; Atchison, Kansas
Jo Ann Radetic; Washington, Missouri
Bill Rapp; Crete, Nebraska
John Rothwell; Michigan
Jim Schaid; AIA
Sally Schwenk; Independence, Missouri
Norbert Shaklette; Villa Ridge, Missouri
John Snyder; Cal Trans, Sacramento, California
Bill Staedler; Railroad Engineer
Eileen Starr; State Historic Preservation Office, Cheyenne, Wyoming
Elaine Ulibarri; Nevada Northern Railway, East Ely, Nevada
Dave Wescock, Nebraska Central
Kyle Wyatt; Nevada State Historical Railroad Museum, Carson City, Nevada

JACKSON.
No Parking
No Parking

A curious and wonderful thing has been happening over the last twenty or thirty years: we Americans have quietly, effectively, begun to husband our heritage in thousands of places and in dozens of ways. It wasn't long ago that an old building was an endangered building, no matter what its pedigree or its accomplishments. George Washington's Mt. Vernon home was once a candidate for demolition. It was saved, but tens of thousands of other structures have been torn down in the name of progress.

But that kind of progress stopped long ago, and we have progressively campaigned to save all sorts of remaining buildings, including many of America's railroad depots. This is a quiet success story, the gradual campaign to insure the preservation of significant buildings, public and private, all across the American landscape. The preservation movement is a public-private partnership that preserves, protects, and defends all kinds of buildings in all sorts of places.

In many American communities the railroad depot was the most important building in town. More than the court house, the school, the hospital, or the mansion on the hill, the depot touched the lives of people in the community. It was the portal to the rest of the world for people out on the Nebraska prairie or along the coast of Maine. It took whatever you had to sell off to market, it brought back whatever you wanted to buy. Everything that was important to a community—people, information, products, coin of the realm—came and went through America's railroad depots.

One authoritative source noted that approximately 140,000 railroad depots have been built in America, most of them in a span of about eighty years, from about 1850 to 1930. A substantial portion were depot replacements, structures built to replace depots lost to fire, flood, and other natural dis-

This fine old depot was built in Jackson, Michigan, in 1876 on the corner of Michigan Avenue and Milwaukee Street. It hadn't been very long since this part of the world was the frontier, but the railroad helped change that. Most of the community of 1876 Jackson is gone, but the old depot lingers on thanks to the cooperative efforts of Amtrak, the state, and local citizens. The building was restored in 1978 and continues to serve rail passengers daily. *Robert Genat*

Right: This old MKT (Missouri-Kansas-Texas Railroad—the "Katy") depot, too good to tear down, was rescued from oblivion by a beverage distributor who moved it across Texas and restored it to its pristine original condition, inside and out. The only thing that would make it really authentic would be a set of tracks outside—but the rails never came within miles of this spot. While some preservationists might scoff, the alternative has been a pile of rubble and a match for thousands of similar little unpretentious depots destroyed over the past few decades.

Below: Yonder comes the train, just as it has for 150-plus years in the United States and Canada.

asters. Another group of replacements covered structures that were rebuilt to replace a worn-out or inadequate smaller building. Some major American cities built three or four depots on the same site as the city grew and became more prosperous.

Most of these structures are gone, and the railway rights-of-way have been abandoned. The American frontier created hundreds of buildings and towns in the last century to suit a particular function, and when the function changed, the structure had to change, too. America has moved very quickly from an agricultural nation to a technological one, from rural farm life to urban city life, from depending on mass transit such as railroads to using personal transportation—the automobile. So it is only reasonable to expect that depots and railroads would mirror this trend away from small towns.

Depots and Railroad's Today

We looked at depot inventories in several states to see how many depots survived. The state of Kansas presents a typical profile. Kansas probably had, in its railroad lifetime, over 1,000 depots. This includes both passenger and freight depots, serving communities along its main line and trunk railways. (Remember some larger communities had more than one depot.) Today Kansas has about 140 depot structures remaining, more than 100 of these have been moved from their original site. Approximately 30 structures are still in some sort of railway use, most as railroad offices or storage buildings. Railroad passengers are actually served at 5 depots; all of them are Amtrak stations. Clearly, depot heritage is less than it once was.

The railroad industry itself, once the largest employer in the United States, has been shrinking since 1930. The private automobile, the airplane and telecommunications networks now provide Americans with the services once provided solely via the railroad. Mail service, freight and parcel delivery, long distance pipelines, and telegraphic services have each grown into separate and distinct major industries.

This leaves the railroad with its own unique niche; very heavy and very bulky commodities, usually raw materials, delivered over very long distances. The railroads can provide transport economically because of the size of the deliveries; it's still cheaper to provide crates of oranges to New York by boxcar than to deliver them to market by truck or plane. And it seems to leave the railroads to handle another commodity they service better than any other network: the daily commuter. Railroads seem to operate faster, easier, and with greater reliability in bad weather than any other form of transportation.

The growth of the railroads is the story of the westward expansion, the story's of America's eco-

nomic development and a singular factor in the rapid rise of American industry. Railroads made it possible to haul bulk commodities around America, precious metals from Nevada, cattle from Texas, coal and iron ore from Wisconsin, timber from Oregon. So this book looks at some of the remaining depots, all of them interesting artifacts of a unique American experience.

The Ogden, Utah, Union Station is an inspiration and a model for other large cities with a deteriorating depot and a dying downtown. Restored in the early 1970s, it was designed by the Parkinsons, a father and son architectural team from Los Angeles.

WOODRIDGE
Cleanser
NATIONAL
BISCUIT
COMPANY

INTRODUCTION

The Day the Railroad Came to Town

The railroad finally came to our hometown on a Saturday afternoon in January of the long ago year of 1864. It was one of those bright, well-scrubbed days that we get out here in San Jose, California, in the winter after a rain—when everything has the clean, clear smell of freshness, promise, and new beginnings. That day, over 130 years past, was obviously a day of new beginnings, and everybody in town knew it. They knew that their world was about to be profoundly changed. When the rain stopped a little after sunrise, the clouds parted and that bright winter sun came out to make everything twinkle... well, everybody was sure it was a good omen. And so it was.

The railroad from San Francisco, fifty miles away up the peninsula, had been planned and promoted ever since 1850, and despite the tremendous costs and complications, the project was well funded and enthusiastically supported by both communities. Over a million dollars had been invested—more than enough to do the job. Even though the Civil War was in full swing, diverting men, materiel, and money, the line was surveyed, graded, and built in just a couple of years. Three locomotives were ordered from the East. They came around the Horn aboard sailing ships in pieces, a six-month journey, then were reassembled, tested, and prepared for service. Even before the line was complete, freight service began on the northern end of the tracks, at an immediate profit.

Even then San Francisco was a city without visible means of support—a raucous, bawdy place whose business was business in

Perhaps the elegantly dressed lady is meeting a special passenger, or maybe she will just travel a short distance. If she were taking a long trip today, she would probably be wearing a long coat, or duster, to keep the particles of oily soot from her dress. Railroads were a dirty experience for travelers and depots alike. But this lacy, Victorian Gothic depot, typical of many small town stations in the eastern United States, looks fresh and clean. This Library of Congress photograph was colorized by Bridget Sullivan. *Library of Congress*

all its permutations: a city of financiers, brokers, real estate agents, speculators, procurers, and pimps of all inclinations. It was a decadent place, full of a gleeful humanity, each expecting three squares (or more) every day, a place where every victual, virtue, and vice had to be imported. And when it came to vittles, San Jose was the closest, cheapest source for barley, brandy, wheat, wine, fruit of many kinds, and vegetables just about all year round. San Jose was (and still is) happy to oblige their neighbor's whim—as long as it was for good gold coin.

Even then San Jose was a farm town, as it had been since the 1770s and would remain for 200 years. It was dedicated to wheat, cattle, fruit, vegetables, all in wholesale quantities. The two cities were made for each other—one set of consumers, another set of producers, fifty miles apart, remote and isolated from the rest of the civilized world.

The only practical form of communication between the two before that day in 1864 was an all-day steamboat ride on the bay or an all-day stage coach ride up the dirt road left over from the Spanish days, the muddy track called El Camino Real. You could ride a horse, and some did, or you could walk, but that took two days. Any of these alternatives was bumpy and exhausting, and the stage and the steam boat were expensive.

The railroad had been around back East for thirty years by then, even longer in England. Every man, woman, and child present in every nook and cranny of America knew about the power of steam. They knew that it had transformed much of the East, where most of them had been born and reared. They had read the wonderful accounts of rapid travel between distant cities, and low fares for shipping commodities and other goods. And they knew, through the newspapers received by ship—only six months late—that all across the East new tracks were being laid and new services were being developed. The train, in other words, was all the rage.

One of the things that motivated these people was their sense of isolation from the rest of America. San Francisco and San Jose were both up-to-date towns, rich in every way, but isolated from each other and from the East. People in both places had money, energy, a sense of purpose, and a vision of linking their cities with the other cities of the United States. They had enough money to buy the best of anything available—including, the communities decided, a railroad.

There were two false starts on the project, but in 1862—with over a million dollars in a construction fund—it began. By 1864 the right of way was prepared, the rails laid, the engines bought, the cars built, the schedules published, the contracts signed, and the deed was done, all in efficient, well-funded order.

Everybody knew the railroad would transform their world, although not everybody agreed just how. As usual, some forecast gloom and doom; others saw only success. Both, as it turned out, were right. On that glittering Saturday morning, the 16th of January 1864, everything was still speculation. But the citizens of San Jose and San Francisco were speculating that it was going to be wonderful!

A few weeks before the grand inauguration, the Board of Directors of the fledgling railroad was assembled and were loaded aboard a wood flat car behind one of the new locomotives—none of the passenger cars were ready for service as yet. These notables in their finery were seated upon wooden benches nailed to the flatcar. Then, with a toot, off they all went.

Previous page: The depot was often the site of community gatherings of all sorts, some happy and others sorrowful. These people have come to grieve for Santa Fe engineer Joe Williams and his fireman, a man named Whittaker, who were murdered by a bandit in Saginaw Hill, Texas, on July 22, 1898. The Santa Fe provided the funeral train and services for the men, free of charge, as the final part of their benefits package. *Atchison, Topeka, and Santa Fe-Kansas State Historical Society*

Wichita, Kansas, 1880. Rail service made this and thousands of other towns possible and were major direct and indirect contributors to the local economy. *Atchison, Topeka, and Santa Fe*

It was, as they say, a learning experience. This little "consist" of one locomotive and tender and one flatcar-load of rich, influential citizens worked its way out of the margins of San Francisco's Mission district, up a long hill and down the other side, then south through the open grassland of the

This simple, unpretentious depot at Santa Clara, California, dates to 1864, making it one of the oldest in the nation still in service and probably the oldest still serving west of the Mississippi. Sixty-two trains stop here every week day, just as trains have since the day it opened for business over 130 years ago. Although the depot hasn't changed much, its presence changed the ground around it.

rural Peninsula. It must have been quite a sight—and an incredible experience.

None of these men had ever traveled faster than a horse could gallop—about seventeen miles an hour—and that for only brief periods. But about ten miles out of town the engineer started to open the throttle. The train picked up speed; twenty miles an hour was an astonishing speed at the time, but that was quickly achieved, then bettered. Thirty, forty, then fifty miles per hour were announced from the cab. The august gentlemen of the Board of Directors knew, of course, that such speeds were possible—but none had ever experienced them! They clutched cigars in tightly-clenched teeth and clamped hats to heads while waiting for the boiler to blow or some other disaster—and they prayed. Their reward was even more speed—sixty miles per hour for a long, fifteen-mile stretch. Then, at last, the gallant engineer eased his throttle, slowed the great engine, and halted at the small town of San Mateo.

The survivors were all duly returned to The City after a day of fun, excitement, and (based on what we already know about this gaggle of gentlemen) large quantities of booze and expensive seegars. Their excitement was electric. Limited service began on the northern part of the line while construction proceeded south at a rapid pace. Soon San Francisco was abuzz with talk of the imminent inauguration of service on the new rail line all the way to San Jose.

It rained during the night before, but the clouds parted that day, over 130 years ago. The sparkling new locomotives were fired early, oiled and polished, inspected by their attendants. Then they began to move, backing to the specially prepared cars which were waiting to convey any interested citizens on a free trip down to San Jose and back again.

The crowds started forming early, too. The officials thought a few hundred people might like a ride—but two or three times as many formed up at the station—the ladies in their fashionable skirts and bonnets, the men in frock coats and stove-pipe hats. There were rough miners, rich matrons, household servants, prostitutes, journalists, men, women, and children—the entire community, jammed together in one squirming, egalitarian, odiferous assembly. The tension grew with the crowd. In the distance they could all hear the chuffing and the little musical toots of the whistle, the ringing of the bell—yet none of them knew just what it was signaling. They heard the boom

The Santa Clara station is certainly among the oldest in the nation, but it otherwise resembles a very common breed and buildings like this could once be found in any part of the country. It is of "board and batten" construction, and its builders would probably be amused at its longevity and the honor it today receives. It was originally built of redwood, one of the reasons for its longevity.

and clatter of the cars as the train was assembled. Then finally, they began to see the iron fire-breathing monster moving back toward the depot. They could feel the very earth quiver beneath their toes, and, with much ceremony and apprehension, the cars were at last moored along side the unfinished Valencia Street passenger depot... and the crowd mobbed the train.

It was obvious to everybody that the available cars couldn't begin to accommodate all the thrill-seekers on the platform. For a moment or two, women and very young children had priority, and several of the cars filled with these fair creatures and their fashionable dresses. Then the men, in all their variety said, "The hell with it," and rushed the other cars, jamming aboard so tightly that it was hard to breathe. Those aboard had to endure the polite fury of those left behind, but they did so without a lot of guilt.

The railroad officials scurried to find more cars. Rough flat cars and gondolas designed for hauling dirt and rocks were produced, and these too quickly filled with human cargo. The first train departed at the scheduled hour of 10 a.m., packed with delighted, apprehensive humanity.

With bells ringing, whistles blasting, with huzzahs and hoorays, children crying and women squealing, these steaming, snorting monsters chuffed out of the depot. They maintained a slow, walking pace through the muddy streets, past the outskirts, past the cheering bystanders. The pace increased; soon these privileged citizens experienced for the first time a sense of speed that they had only heard reported.

At stations along the route, Redwood City, San Mateo, and others—were crowds of people, all in their finery, hoping the train would stop and invite them aboard—and all were disappointed. With a blast of the whistle, a ring of the bell, the locomotives thundered past while the human cargo cheered, and those who could move an arm waved a greeting.

Fifty miles south of San Francisco, the assembled citizens (honorable and otherwise) of San Jose stood anxiously waiting on the platform of the new station. A small band provided by the California Guards artillery formed up early, brought their tubas and coronets to parade rest and stood by for action. Most had never actually seen a train, although many had read about them. Some had traveled for days to witness the

Depots had many functions and many specialized fixtures. Here is a dispenser for tickets and timetables. The depot was much more than the four walls alongside the track—whole industries evolved to design and construct the many specialized items needed by such places.
Ralph Domenici collection

event; elegant Mexican Dons with immense ranchos, Chinese laborers, immigrants from Ireland, France, England, Chile, Samoa. Most had only recently spent months of hazardous travel aboard sailing ships or conestoga wagons or on horseback to get to this promised land, and this new technology, each knew, promised a radical change in the fates and fortunes of them all.

The first train pulled up to the new depot at Santa Clara, less than three miles from San Jose at 11:30, half an hour before the scheduled grand arrival. Since the two trains were to arrive at the ceremony together, the first had to wait for the second to catch up; passengers were invited to pry themselves from their perches and stretch their legs for a few minutes. Many wandered over to inspect the ancient mission and visit the university while others studied the new depot, water tower, and furnishings recently installed by the railroad company. All present agreed that the trip had thus far been a perfect marvel.

The second train arrived with a toot, received a toot salute in return, and both processions steamed off for the last, short leg of the journey together, just as advertised. It was quite a party. The band played, then the speakers spoke, then everybody adjourned to assemble lunch from a buffet 100 feet long. The consensus, both from the parade of distinguished speakers and the crowd too, was that this was the opening of an entirely new epoch. Then they got back on the trains and went home.

Well, they were right, and all the predictions started coming true almost immediately. The next day the steamboats announced a cut in the fare between the two cities from $10 to $5, although the boats still took all day to make the trip. The railroad began regular passenger and freight service; the fare was $4 each way and the fifty-mile journey took only about an hour and a half. Steamboats quickly went out of the passenger business between the two communities.

The line started making money immediately—lots of money. Both cities immediately began to profit from the new form of communication. Every little crossroad village where the new train stopped began to prosper and grow. Simple, unpretentious depots sprouted along the tracks about every eight miles or so, with flag stops in between.

Of course the skeptics and nay-sayers were right, too. The locomotives scared the horses until they got used to the routine, and sparks set fire to the ripening grain alongside the tracks later in the spring. The bucolic environment between the two communities started to change, and that lovely rural life was gradually doomed. Then in 1869, five years after the line opened, the transcontinental railroad was completed and the West and the East were finally stitched firmly together.

Well, that was a long time ago. Almost every thing those people knew has changed in the 130 years since that happy, sparkling day when the railroad first began to serve and change these two towns. The names of the two communities remain, but nearly everything in them and between them has been changed in profound ways. Those two steel rails, the locomotives that roll on them, and the depots where the trains start and stop are fundamentally responsible.

We selected this story about San Jose because our hometown isn't really special or unique—it was typical in how towns grew and were affected by the coming of the rails. Back in the 1860s this story was repeated in dozens of places, with identical particulars. The names of the towns and the names of the railroads were different, but the process was the same. The arrival of the railroad and the appearance of a new depot changed every town. And in many places out West, the railroad depot was the beginning of the town. It started about 1860 and continued for about forty years. The railroad became the veins and arteries, then the capillaries, bringing and taking the lifeblood of culture and commerce to the most remote corners of the continent.

The depots were of all sizes, shapes, and styles. There were tiny little shelter sheds and way stations, there were ornate gothic, gingerbread confections, there were the towering terminals like Grand Central and the other Union Stations. For a period of about ninety years the passenger railroad network developed, then declined. Now, of course, all that is long in the past, and we're supposed to tell you that progress has bypassed the railroad era and all it accomplished. Despite what so many people seem to think however, it isn't true.

Above: Tonkawa, Oklahoma. Another example of the cheap, simple, unpretentious little depots installed every five or ten miles along the line during the days when railroads transformed the American landscape.

A waiting room sign, perhaps the original, from the 1864 depot at Santa Clara. This is now part of the museum collection at the Santa Clara depot.

It's hard to tell from old black and white photographs just how bright and lively the people and the machines of 1864 appeared at the time, but this will give you some clues. It was common for locomotives to be adorned and embellished with bright red paint, gold leaf, and plenty of decorative pin-striping. Here you see Jupiter on the approximate spot where the east and west rails were finally joined at Promontory, Utah, in 1869.

The passenger train still runs forty-seven miles from San Francisco down to San Jose and back again—sixty two times a day. Hundreds of passengers board the train at our old Santa Clara depot every day, headed for jobs, shopping, or just to ride the train. It still takes an hour and a half to go from San Jose to San Francisco—just as in 1864—and it still costs about $5 each way. As the farmers predicted, the farms along the old El Camino Real are gone. In their place are cities and towns, all born and nurtured by the iron horse and the commerce in products and ideas. Each of these places was and is nourished by the rails, and each has its little palace dedicated to the iron god: the depot.

Well, the first depot in San Francisco has been replaced several times, and the one here in San Jose where folks first celebrated so gleefully that day in 1864 is gone, too. But the one at Santa Clara—that simple board and batten building where the crowds detrained to stretch their legs 130 years ago—still stands and is still in business. It is as plain and sturdy as a barn, with lines to match. People arrive every morning, buy their tickets from the station agent inside, assemble at trackside, and wait for the train to San Francisco. Every evening those same people step down from the 5:10 or the 6:35. The old mission is still just across the road, much older now, and the university is much larger. A major airport a mile or so to the east has replaced the depot as the primary port of entry for travelers from distant places. The

wheat fields and pastures that surrounded this simple depot have had homes and businesses on them since the 1870s, but the depot is unchanged—it is even the same color. It is one thing the ghosts of that inaugural day would recognize immediately.

That depot at Santa Clara changed the town in which it stood. It was a portal to another world. As a direct result of this simple structure and the rails alongside, a city grew. Without the depots and rails, the cities of Santa Clara and San Jose would still be remote little farm towns, like so many others bypassed by the train.

The Santa Clara depot is special in one respect, and that is its age. During the 1860s, '70s, '80s, and '90s, there were hundreds of such buildings assembled everywhere in the United States and Canada. They were simple, unpretentious structures made of painted wood, cheap board-and-batten constructions. They weren't expected to last forever, and most disappeared long ago, with few tears shed.

The railroads built so many of them that the designs were standardized. They were designated Common Standard Design No.1, No.2, or No.3. They came in sizes from little to large. A typical small depot was like the 9ft by 34ft structure the Kansas City, Mexico & Orient built to serve West Wichita, Kansas. It took a week to assemble, between the 9th and 19th of August, 1912, at a total cost of $347.17. There were others, sprouting across the American landscape like so many mushrooms, with about as much variety. Many

Promontory, Utah. Well, it wasn't much of a depot, but there wasn't all that much business in town, either. In fact, there wasn't much of a town and railroad traffic took an easier route within a year or two. But the abandoned Promontory station remained for years after the Golden Spike was driven before the last of the shacks finally disintegrated.

Depots were stylish and well-appointed? Yes, some were. Yet in the early days, and sometimes later as well, depots were often stark, simple enclosures, as plain and sturdy and unpretentious as a barn. This combination depot served passengers in one end, freight in the other. The Union Pacific still uses this one in Denton, Texas, although the passing trains don't bring passengers here any more.

Here is the Atchison part of the famous Atchison, Topeka, and Santa Fe. Although the tracks out front are still active, you can't board the train here—it stops only occasionally, many miles away. But you can learn a lot about them here because this 1880s depot building, like so many others, has been saved by conversion to a museum.

were precut at a factory, shipped to their destinations on one or more flat cars, and assembled on site in a few days or a week.

These depots were installed across the country as quickly as the roadbed was graded and the rails were laid. Across Ohio, Illinois, Iowa, Nebraska, and Wyoming, you can still see where they once were; the original depots are virtually all gone, and sometimes the railroads with them, but their legacy lives on in the little communities, about seven miles apart, that grew around the little country depots. The Santa Clara depot is special since it is rare survivor of this early group of depots. That's not a bad accomplishment for something built of simple redwood boards, assembled in a few days.

For the communities that grew up around the depots, these little buildings were the portal to the whole wide world. Every dusty, barefoot street urchin knew that adventure and opportunity were available just by going in that door, buying a ticket, and getting on the next train to the big city. Many of these urchins did precisely that at the first opportunity—without even bothering with the ticket simply by sneaking a ride on a passing train.

These depots were portals in two directions—coming and going. Through the depot you shipped your wheat, barley, pigs, horses, and cattle to markets and to buyers hundreds of miles away. That was a profound change in the business of farming. You shipped your daughters off to college and your boys off to war; you went off to visit, and people came to visit you. This was a profound change in the ways people viewed and used their

Denton, Texas. The Union Pacific was trying to get rid of this building when this photograph was made, intending to let the city move it away from the tracks for a museum or other function—otherwise the railroad wanted to tear it down.

Upper left: The idea that form ought to follow function was not widely accepted in the 1870s when this ceiling was installed in a simple little railroad building at Atchison, Kansas. Depots and most other railroad structures were built to work, but they were also built to entertain the eye and mind, too. This pressed tin ceiling is in a bridge-tender's building that still does the work it was intended to do about 120 years ago.

Upper right: Freight room, Denton, Texas. There's an old railroad tradition that calls for every depot employee to "sign in" when they're hired on and to "sign out" when they leave, and those signatures here go back to about the First World War.

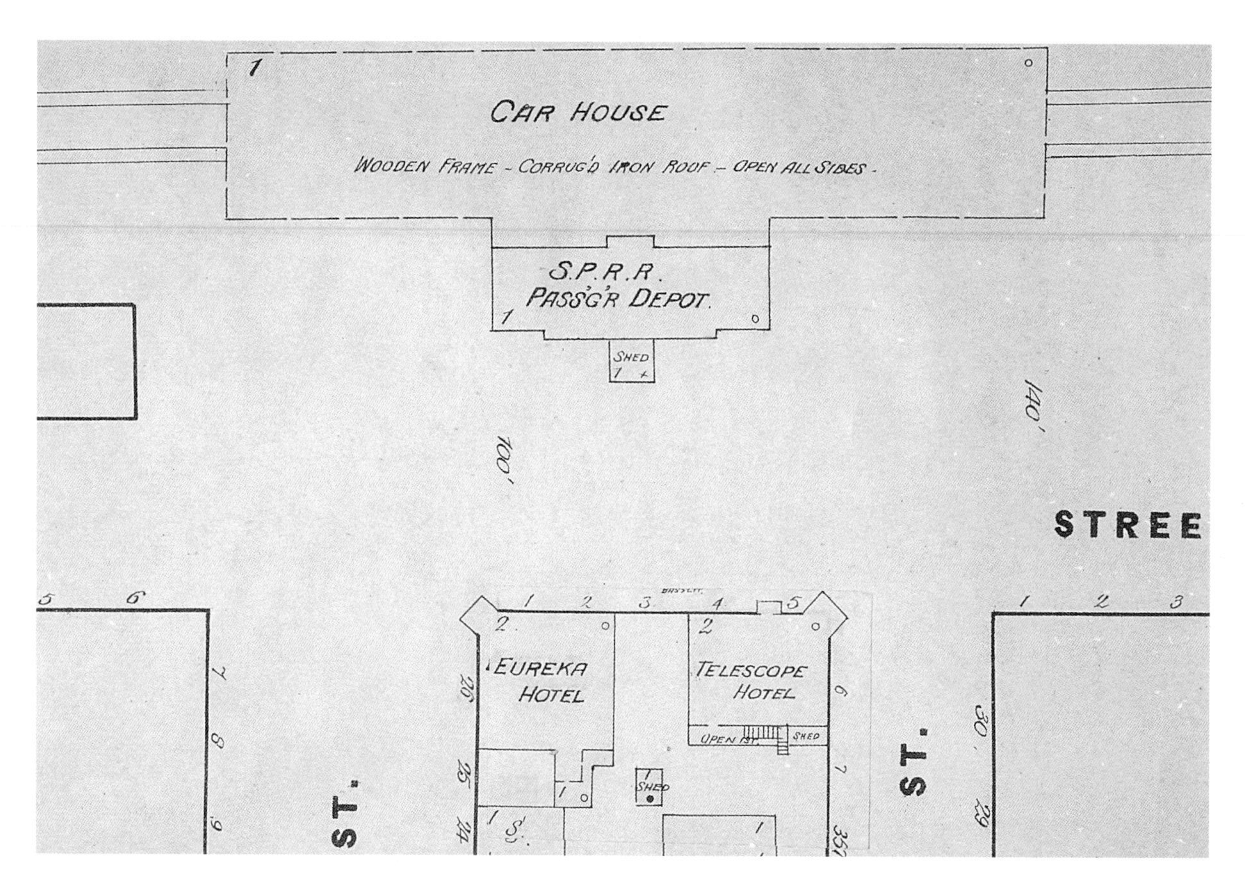

Right: A Sanborn insurance map, circa 1890, shows the original San Jose, California, depot. A train shed covers arriving and departing passengers on the platforms behind the depot. Across the street, an easy walk for anyone, two hotels are ready to accommodate travelers. *Franklin Maggi collection*

world, and in the size and shape of their personal universe.

Through the depot, coming back from those distant cities, came brides and bicycles, gold coin, daily newspapers, the catalogues from Sears Roebuck and Montgomery Ward... the latest fashions in plows, harrows, and grain harvesting machines; skirts, hats, blouses, cloth by the yard, and sewing machines and patterns for men's, ladies', and children's apparel; caskets, and embalming kits; saws, wrenches, carpentry tools for any application; harnesses for horses and mules; buggies, surreys, broughams, and sturdy farm wagons; steam fire engines weighing eight tons; letters from friends in Sweden, Germany, Russia, and Ireland.

Off the train at the depot came the people who made America: the preachers and prostitutes, the farmers and mechanics, teamsters and the U.S. marshals, the cowboys, crooks, and the cops; the wives and the husbands, and large gaggles of children of all breeds and conformance. There were regiments of traveling salesmen. Prostitutes quickly began using the train as the basis for a circuit, moving from one city to another every few months, when they discovered that a new face in a community was a marketable commodity.

Now, a lot of those little depots are gone, and some of the communities that grew up around them are gone as well. Both the depots and the towns became obsolete, dried up, and blew away. Some railroads, like the Burlington Northern, have gone down the line, systematically bulldozing their quaint little depots, one after the other. Iowa, where dozens of these little depots once punctuated the landscape, is now mostly barren of them. The depots are gone. They served their function, lived their productive lives, and died a natural death.

Many of us love our rail heritage and some of us lament the loss of its mythical, romantic past. There are a lot of folks who still haven't quite accepted the idea that the day of the steam locomotive is really over, for example, and there are groups of people who lament the loss of every single little crossroad station. It is amazing and wonderful that we preserve and protect so many of these old, frail, obsolete buildings. There are thousands of depots still around although only a small number still serve passengers. People love these buildings so much that they are preserved spontaneously, in dozens of ways, long after any other structure would be demolished without regret.

There's a little country depot alongside the road between Abilene and Sweetwater, Texas, that is in pristine condition; it glitters in fresh paint and wears the emblem of the Missouri-Kansas-Texas Rail Road under its generous, shady eaves. But the MKT never came near this isolated spot, and the depot was imported from hundreds of miles west. It was purchased by a beverage distribution company, trucked from its original site, and restored to new condition for use as offices.

In fact, you quickly learn to sense where a depot belongs in a community, and you can drive to the spot—sight unseen—and there it will be! Sometimes it is empty, often it will serve a new function, but you can drive from Atlantic to Pacific along the old roads, the ones that follow the rails, and in town after town you can find the old depot like a bird dog finds a pheasant—almost by sense of smell.

Depot agents had many responsibilities, including the keys for all sorts of locks that secured switches, signals, freight, and currency in and around the depot. This "heart" style lock was manufactured under contract to the Western Pacific railroad about 1900.

They aren't always alongside the tracks anymore, and they aren't always in pristine condition but many are still standing—and frequently groups of people are working to preserve them, one way or another. Some are pizza parlors, restaurants, museums, or feed stores. Many are abandoned. But huge numbers are alive in one form or another, long after civic contemporaries were torn down for something more modern. Given a chance, Americans prefer their depots right where they belong, beside the tracks serving passengers. But when that isn't possible, communities all over the country start petitions, take up collections, and pitch in to save these buildings in any way they can—even if that means turning them into a museum, chamber of commerce, or real estate office.

A few huge depots, like St. Louis' glorious Union Station, have been preserved, even if only as a hotel. Washington, D. C.'s Union Station has been renovated at tremendous cost, and so have many others. There are also dozens—maybe hundreds—of major depots that still serve their communities for rail travel, just as they were intended, fifty or seventy years ago. Ogden, Utah, has one of these depots, and Sacramento, California, has another. Cincinnati, Hoboken, San Diego, and many other communities have preserved their depots by using them as rail passenger depots. Many de-

Perhaps your grandparents or great-grandparents clutched one of these cheap immigrant tickets that brought our ancestors from Russia, Sweden, Ireland, Poland, France, and all the other places to new homes in the promised land: to Minnesota, Nebraska, the Dakota territory, California, Oregon, or as in this case, from Chicago to Iowa. Immigrants rode in cold, plain, slow cars, and were sometimes accommodated in separate waiting rooms, but the fare was dirt cheap and sometimes free. *Ed Peterman collection*

An Amtrak train stops in front of the delicious Kirkwood, Missouri, depot outside St. Louis. Amtrak achieved what was once thought impossible, the resurrection of passenger rail service to many parts of the United States. Amtrak takes a lot of criticism from some of the railfan community for the horrid little "Amshack" shelters sometimes provided instead of a real depot, but the corporation also sinks millions annually into the old depots, too.

pots combine local light rail and long distance rail service.

So the story of the rail passenger depot in the United States is still evolving because passenger rail travel is once again growing and changing. There is enough rail traffic that in 1993, a brand new replacement passenger depot was opened in Emeryville, California. Other depots are being reconditioned and restored all over the country. Although some wonderful buildings have been destroyed over the past few decades, many more have been saved and many others are in a state of suspended decay, waiting for their communities to either preserve or discard them. This book is the story of all of them, great and small, grand and humble.

Right: The clock tower of Cheyenne, Wyoming's Union Pacific station was designed to be a landmark, and it can be seen for miles before the depot appears. This National Register depot was designed by the architectural firm of Van Brunt and Howe, after years of lobbying and negotiation by Cheyenne citizens.

MILAN
WAITING ROOM

CHAPTER 1

Life at the Depot

Depots and roundhouses are small components of very large systems. In many cases they are all that remain of what were once-thriving rail transport organizations spread across vast spaces. You can't really understand or appreciate a depot or an old roundhouse without having a sense of how the whole organism functioned.

For example, trains don't just push away from the dock and chug off into the sunset. Every train movement is rigidly controlled through formal orders and signals. When a train pulls out of a depot the engineer has a formal set of orders that allow movement only for a few miles, when another set of orders and authority to proceed must be received. This system developed slowly, and at great cost, during the formative years of rail systems, when multiple trains used the same single track in both directions. The depot, the station agent, the signal man, and the telegrapher became essential elements in the control of train movement.

Before this system was developed and adopted, train wrecks were commonplace events, resulting in scandalous loss of life. Many hundreds of people, passengers and crew both, were killed annually during the late 19th century when head-on collisions and other disasters occurred with amazing frequency.

Depots helped reduce that loss. The depot became one node in the control system that developed because the telegraph allowed someone on the depot staff to be in constant communication with stations up and down the line, to report on the progress and posi-

Milan, Missouri's old depot has it all: a little waiting room for passengers on the left, a little freight room on the right, and a little office in the middle for the depot agent to conduct business. The bay window made it a bit easier to see approaching trains from up and down the track.

A little town got a little depot with simple amenities. The waiting room here would accommodate all comers—men, women, immigrants, and even those who were called "colored" in the past. But bigger depots would offer separate facilities for each and insist that everyone knew their place and stayed in it.

tion of every train, and to keep trains safely separated at all times.

Roundhouses & Shops

Alongside many depots are the flip side of the railroad station, the roundhouse and the engine house. Few of these are left, and far fewer become quaint restaurants or hotels. Most are allowed to rot until they fall over, although a few are burned (by accident or design) and others are torn down. Across the tracks from the old Santa Clara, California, depot is the decaying Santa Fe roundhouse, one of only five roundhouses left in the state of California. The locomotives are gone now; it serves hobos and derelicts instead.

That's too bad, but somewhat understandable. These big buildings were designed and built for one function—to provide sheltered space for locomotive maintenance work—and they aren't very adaptable. There are enough of them still around, though, to get a sense of what they once did, of the steamy romances people once had with the glittering, fire-breathing power units of the past. Huge crews of men once labored around the clock to maintain the engines; they, and the story of their day, are mostly forgotten. Forgotten too is the kind of community railroad workers once enjoyed—the days, fifty years and more ago, when roundhouse crews had their own marching bands, their weekly barbecues, their own semi-secret society. Those days are gone, and most of those men, too; but some remain, and a few have stories to tell. And there are a few—a very few—of these places still left in business, where locomotives (steam and diesel) are serviced and maintained. This book is the story of these buildings, too.

Depot Fundamentals: 'Station' vs. 'Depot'

Although the terms are often interchanged, there is an important difference between what a railroad calls a station and what they call a depot. A station is a physical location—perhaps nothing more than a milepost and a sign with a name on it. The Southern Pacific Rule Book definition is "... a place identified by name in the timetable." These places may have a spur track, a corral for unloading livestock, perhaps a freight loading platform, maybe a shelter of some sort, or often a tiny, unattended freight house. But many "stations" never had a place to buy a ticket, wait for a train, or provided a place where passengers were allowed to board. At the other extreme, stations could also be large, elaborate facilities with many different structures, including shops, engine houses, water tanks, freight houses, and passenger depots.

The depot is the building designed to accommodate passengers, freight, or both. In small depots the handling of this cargo, human and otherwise, was often combined. However, "main track" stations often had separate depots for freight and passengers.

Sometimes depots or "train order offices" were built in places where there were neither passengers or freight business, just to have an operator or telegrapher present to pass along train orders. These places could be extremely isolated and remote. Depot his-

torian Henry Bender says, "the depot customarily served two major functions—it helped operate the railroad by coordinating train movements, and it promoted the company's business by selling tickets. There were several ancillary functions too: serving as agencies for railway express, Western Union telegraph services, and others.

"There were three major classes of depots: A, B, and C. The Santa Fe railroad kept rosters of the agents assigned to these depots, and often the Class C depots from around 1900 to 1910 had a woman listed as the agent, although rarely will you find a woman listed as agent at the larger Class B or A depots. Women tended to remain at the same depot, while the men tended to move around a lot more."

For the men, at least, the job involved a lot of mobility. The managers insisted on rapid changes. Many of these agents were assigned to places that would very rarely have a passenger, or any freight business at all. These places were about three to five miles apart, although on some lines the train order offices in particularly remote locations were sometimes twenty to twenty-five miles apart.

Not all depots were staffed around the clock, and at the remote ones the railroad had to provide some sort of housing for the agent, operator, or telegrapher—all of whom were sometimes the same person. Often this housing was a second story on the depot, with a small apartment for the agent and his or her family. If a telegrapher was also assigned to one of these places, he usually got to bunk in a slightly modified boxcar behind out back of the depot.

As Henry Bender says, "The usual perception people have of depots is that they are places where

Much of the manufactured goods that came to Milan in the early decades of this century came to town through that door. Freight business was a major component of the depot's work in any town, big or small, and the depot was designed for freight just as much as for passengers.

A Telegraph Operator's
WORK IS PLEASANT,
pays good wages, and leads to
the highest positions. We teach
it quickly and start our graduates
in telegraph service. Railroads are
very busy. Operators are in great
demand. Write for catalogue.
VALENTINES' SCHOOL OF TELEGRAPHY, Janesville, Wis.

you go to buy your ticket, then sit in the waiting room until it is time for the train to come. There was a lot more to it than that."

Communicating By Telegraph

Depot operators communicated by telegraphy, a skill that was a job requirement in some places right up to the 1980s. Each station had a two-letter identifier, rather like the three-letter identifier airports have today, and each message to a particular depot began with those two letters. It was easy for the telegraphers to identify each other just by listening to the way the dots and dashes were sent—a kind of audible signature called a "hand."

"Trains operated normally by 'time-table' authority," explains Henry Bender. "Most railroads were single tracked, with sidings every twenty miles or so, with a dispatcher somewhere along the line keeping track of where all the trains were, all the time. He did so with a large sheet of paper, called a 'train sheet,' and often a map, although he knew quite well where all the stations were. He kept track of how each train was progressing, and if all the trains went along according to schedule, he knew when, and where they would meet and pass each other.

The telegraph operator was absolutely essential in this system only when one train was delayed, or if an extra train was added to the schedule, or if an extra "section" was added—as often happened—which is when this thing got very complicated and potentially dangerous. When additional sections were added, it was at this point that the telegraphers in their lonely little telegraph offices became real life savers. "Extras" were complete additional trains running in the same slot of the timetable, one behind the other. You might have, say, train #26-1, #26-2, and #26-3 all running a section of track usually occupied only by one train, the normal #26. Each train except the last had to show green flags and green lights on the locomotive and the caboose, indicating that additional sections were following.

"The operator played a critical role, even when there were no extras, by reporting when a train went past the depot by transmitting 'O S' to the dispatcher. OS stands for 'on-sheet', and that would be followed by the station identifier, the number of the train, and the time of the passage," explains Henry Bender. "Odd and even numbers were used to indicate direction—odd for westbound, for example,

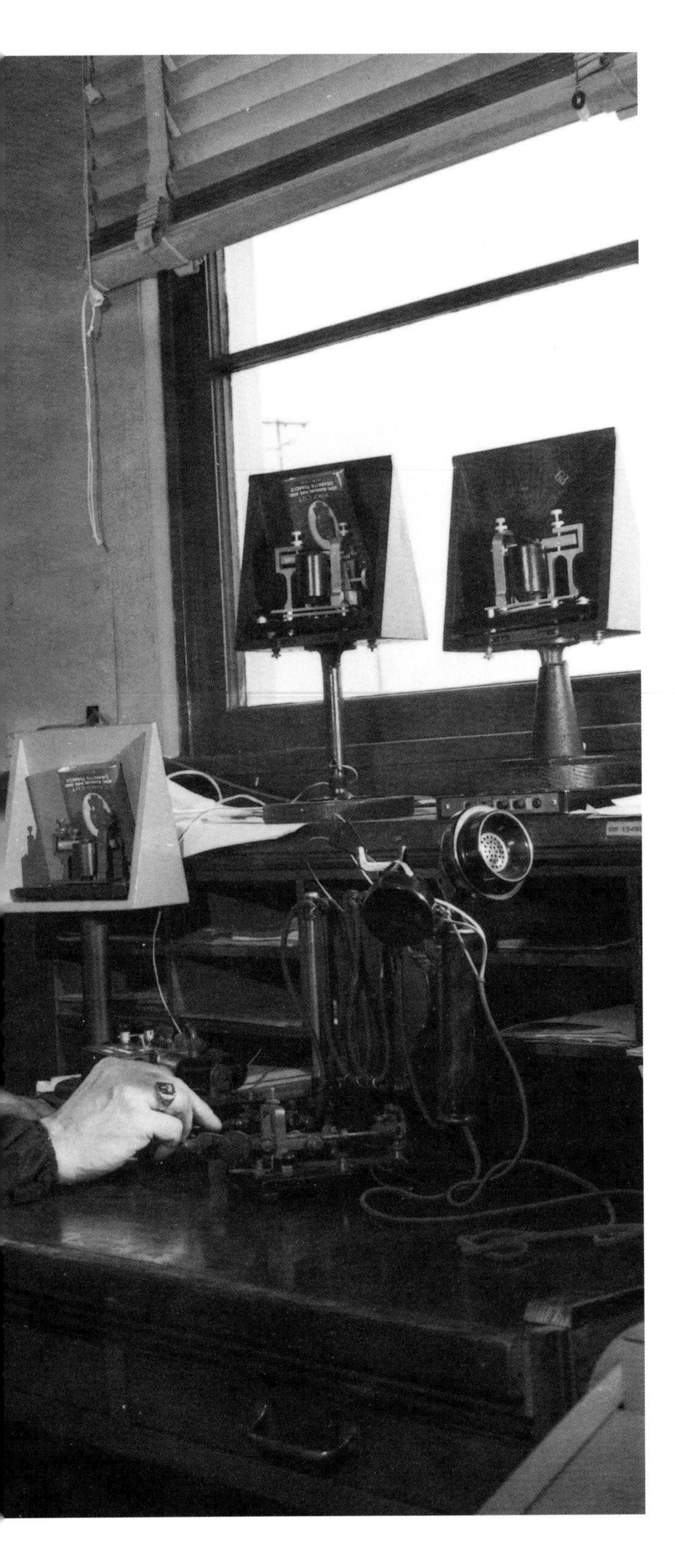

and even for eastbound." The odd-even system continues today in American transportation networks. It is identical to the basis for en-route air traffic control used today to coordinate the movement of airplanes across the world.

Development of the intricate web of rail systems would have been impossible without this system to manage the movement of trains, and the depot operators were crucial links between the dispatchers and the train crews. The depot agent or operator wrote down the train orders as they were received by telegraph, then handed the orders up to the engine crew on arrival at the station. Generally, there were three copies of the order—the original for the train crew, a carbon kept for the dispatcher, and another carbon for the agent's records. Sometimes the train stopped, and the agent and engineer met face-to-face, but often the order was held aloft on a stick and snatched from the agent as the locomotive thundered past at speed.

Left: The Santa Fe's resident "brass-pounder" in Fullerton, California, gossips with somebody down the line. He has customized the sounders of two circuits with Prince Albert pipe tobacco tins (empty), a very common practice. This agent is quite nattily attired in his vest and sleeve protectors, and he has put on his cap for the benefit of the photographer. *Atchison, Topeka, and Santa Fe collection—Kansas State Historical Society*

Until fairly recently, a job requirement for any aspiring depot agent was proficiency in Morse code. With simple instruments like this one agents were able to communicate train orders, news, gossip, personal messages via Western Union, and some even managed to conduct romances along the wires. Each telegrapher's style (or "hand" as it is called) was as distinctive as his or her voice, instantly recognizable to the answering party. This device that appears so simple and crude in comparison to our modern systems was part of the technological revolution that swept America after the Civil War. It was a marvel in its time, and with it people accomplished marvelous things. *South Bay Historical Railroad collection*

This exchange of orders was an important formality. For some (called "nineteen" orders) the engineer train was signaled to halt the train and actually sign for the receipt of the document. Others, called "thirty-one" orders, could be picked up on the fly, usually by the fireman, who had to lean out and snag a hoop held up by the agent on the ground. After the successful delivery of the order, the agent telegraphed back to the dispatcher to report that the train order had actually been given to the train crew.

When the telephone was introduced, beginning in the 1880s, it supplemented rather than replaced the telegraph, and it took 100 years to fully displace the earlier technology. The last of the California telegraph train order offices didn't convert from this system of delivering train orders until

The Santa Fe depot staff in Lubbock, Texas, 1911. A depot might be staffed (they would have said "manned" even if it were by a woman) one or many people—including one to three telegraphers, an agent, a baggage agent, and perhaps an assistant or two. In really small depots, though, the agent, telegrapher, ticket seller, and baggage handler was likely to be one man or woman who did it all. *Atchison, Topeka, and Santa Fe collection—Kansas State Historical Society*

the 1980s, when direct radio communication between the train crew and the dispatcher finally eliminated the last of the lonely operators and their remote little depots.

There were many stations that existed only to serve this communication function, where there was no community anywhere nearby, and sometimes virtually no other human beings within miles.

Depot Daily Life

The routine for a station varied with the size of the staff and amount of traffic, but some things were pretty much unavoidable everywhere. One of these was paperwork.

There was paperwork for just about everything. When a railroad worker had been absent from the depot for an extended period, a whole set of documents had to be filled out and signed upon their return. Every depot had a revolver, stored in the drawer under the counter, and a receipt for it had to be signed; part of the job description for the agent included shooting it out with robbers. There was a lot of cash to be accounted for in many stations, and the US Mail and Railway Express also required detailed bookkeeping. Once each day a form was completed by the agent listing the number of passenger tickets sold, the amount of each ticket, and the total money received. Then,

monthly summary reports had to be prepared, also on company forms.

Besides the paperwork, agents made routine weather observations and reported them by telegraph—temperature, wind speed and direction, barometric pressure—all sent in daily to the dispatcher or railroad weather office. Such information was considered essential because it helped the railroad anticipate the need for crews to repair wash-outs and clear snow.

The agent at each station, no matter how small or remote, had tremendous responsibility and authority. The boss of each was the designated agent, man or woman. He or she issued orders, distributed payroll, and performed what amounted to about a dozen separate functions. Some of the collateral jobs, though, paid extra money, one of the things that made the position of station agent a valuable one.

For example, many railroad station agents were also representatives for Wells Fargo Railway Express Agency and Western Union. Although the work was accomplished on what appeared to be railroad company time, and using railroad company facilities, the agents were paid independently—and they made a lot of extra income.

The Lonedale Operator

Many train order stations were established in places where there was no town, no people, no traffic, and no company whatever. These little depots had an essential function, but were sometimes very difficult to keep staffed because of the isolation. For operators at these remote offices there was no communication with anyone except by telegraph or telephone. The frequent result was that, after a week or two, the operator quit.

Reading Railroad depot, Myerston, Pennsylvania, about 1915. The semaphore signal on the bracket above the bay window was an important technological innovation when it finally received universal acceptance in the 1880s, about the time this pretty little depot was built. The semaphores were each controlled by a lever on the operator's table below, advising the train crew to stop. *Library of Congress*

Controlling switches and signals was the biggest responsibility for many depot agents in the old days of "train order control." Until fifty years ago each small segment of track had its own local agent to control the movement of trains. Today, though, these switches and signals are controlled by people many miles away, working with computers and communicating with trains by radio. That conversion, as much as anything, eliminated the need for the thousands of simple little depots that once were so common.

This was one reason for the conversion from train order control to centralized train control (CTC), the system that allowed the dispatcher to control all the switches and signals from a central office. When CTC was developed, the need for many of the tiny stations and their telegraphers was over.

But the old system was still in place during World War II and the railroads had to scramble to find people to staff the thousands of little remote stations. Many had little training, even less experience,

Above left: Here's another example of the bay window; this one belongs to the very handsome stone-and-tile depot in Grand Junction, Colorado. Although it appears to be in poor condition, this sturdy old building is about to be restored to its original glory.

Above right: San Carlos, California. No matter how grand or humble, depots serving small communities were built with a bay window for the agent-telegrapher to see trains approaching and departing. This delicious building dates to 1888 and still serves hundreds of commuter passengers daily. The small window in the center allowed the agent to pass orders to train crews without having to leave his desk.

Learning the Code

In the early days, the middle to late 1800s, men learned telegraphy by just hanging around the depot, listening and watching and asking questions of the telegrapher. If the local telegrapher happened to be a friendly character he might take an interested pupil under his wing, teaching the code and explaining the routine. Later, formal schools for telegraphers were established by the railroads.

Over the years a number of charming traditions evolved among the fraternity of telegraphers. One, for example, was a set of "shorthand" codes for common expressions; "73" was understood by all to represent a cordial closing, warm regards. Another was the tradition for telegraphers to chat with each other, up and down the line. Since some of these telegraphers were unattached and lonesome young men and women, it was inevitable that romances developed along the wires, even with other stations listening in.

Thomas Alva Edison was one of those who learned the job in the informal way, along with others who later rose to prominence. It was a job that demanded integrity, intelligence, and a certain amount of what was called "spunk" back then.

"There must have been a few dishonest characters among the agents," Henry Bender says, "but I don't know of any. This is in contrast with the reputation of railroad conductors, where a certain amount of graft was almost expected. Conductors routinely pocketed a portion of the receipts for tickets sold to passengers aboard the trains."

WELCOME TO JACKSON
FROM
EXPECTED
FROM THE WEST
FROM THE EAST
GRAND RAPIDS BRANCH
SAGINAW BRANCH
MEN

Previous page: Jackson, Michigan. These benches were designed to be comfy, but not too comfy to discourage people from sleeping on them.
Robert Genat

A hundred years of use hasn't managed to destroy these sturdy old benches in the Jackson, Michigan, depot. They still accommodate about 33,000 passengers every year.
Robert Genat

and sometimes virtually no idea of the conditions under which they would live and work.

Dick Maurer's Second Trick

Dick Maurer went to work for Southern Pacific in 1942, first as a clerk at the company headquarters in San Francisco. Southern Pacific operated a school for novice telegraphers at night and Dick took the six-month course, graduating in October of 1942. "Besides telegraphy, we learned all the aspects of the agent's job: you had to know the rule book, the proper method of copying down train orders, and all the other details."

His name went up on the "extra board" along with all the other people without permanent assignments. "I broke in at Red Bluff, on the Shasta Division, for a week or two," Dick Maurer recalls, "then from there to Algoma, the first station north of Klamath Falls in eastern Oregon. You stayed on the extra board until you had enough seniority to bid on a regular job, but until then, they could send you all over the place. I worked the second 'trick' at Algoma for a couple of months, then from there they sent me to Chamult, Oregon, where the Northern Pacific and the Southern Pacific shared some track. I worked the 'three trick' there, from midnight to eight, then they opened up an office at a siding called Mowich. Our office was an old boxcar that had been taken off its wheels. The office was in one end of the car, in the middle we had a kitchen, then the sleeping quarters for the three of us were on the other end of the car. It wasn't too bad—except that the 'bathroom' was a privy out in the woods, and in wintertime that was cold!"

As in most train order stations, there were three shifts, or "tricks." Trick 1 was the day shift, 8 am to 4 pm; Trick 2 was the swing shift, until midnight; and

Although not often used by the depot agent, velocipedes like this one were once found at many remote stations. With one of these you could travel quickly up and down the track, inspecting right-of-way for problems. This one served until the 1940s. *South Bay Historical Railroad Society collection*

Even towns of modest size often demanded separate facilities for men and women. The men got to smoke and spit and swear, the women got to nurse babies in private. This door is in one of four remaining depots in Leavenworth, Kansas; it is currently in use as a Mexican restaurant but even so is mostly in original condition.

Trick 3 was the graveyard shift from midnight to eight in the morning. The station agent-telegrapher got the first trick, and he was boss of the place.

"There was plenty to keep you busy," Dick says. "Even on the third trick, you had to file the tariffs in the tariff books, in addition to helping with the agent's work. But our main duty was the handling of train orders, receiving them from the dispatcher by telegraph or telephone, typing them on the proper form, then delivering them to the trains."

Train Orders

The train order became an essential document and a precise ritual—and was the forerunner of today's high-altitude en-route air traffic control clearance. The message provided authority to move across a very carefully defined section of track at a given time.

The dispatcher issued each order in a formal way: as he wrote each order in his book as the order was being telephoned or telegraphed to the designated station. Then the designated station had to repeat the order back to the dispatcher, who then underlined each word of the order as it came back over the wire from the operators. This was intended to be a verification that the order was correctly received.

The telegrapher could tell a lot about a train just by its number; on the Southern Pacific line all eastbound trains were even-numbered and westbound were given odd numbers. Freight trains always had a 600-series number, and on the Shasta division, where Dick Maurer worked, freights were in the 620s or 630s. Passenger (or "first class") trains carried low numbers; the Shasta Daylight was No. 9 or No. 10, depending on direction, and the Cascade was either No. 11 or No. 12. Dick has no trouble reciting the numbers of all those long-dead trains fifty years after he handed up their orders. "There were a lot of passenger trains back then," he says.

The message came from the dispatcher and was addressed to a specific train in the person of the conductor and the engineer. Here's what a train order sounded like to the telegrapher or the agent in the depot:

Train Order Number 101, To: C and E, Train Number 623 at Algoma.

Train 623, take siding and meet Train 628 at Chelsea.

Signed, WJM, Chief Dispatcher

"C and E" was understood to mean conductor and engineer and "WJM" was also understood to be the initials of William J. Manley, the chief dispatcher for the whole division.

From the station agent's point of view, there were three normal alternatives for each train coming down the track. If there were no orders at all, the agent changed the train order signal from red to green—but only when he had visual contact with the locomotive and was sure the engineer had a chance to see the red turn to green. The second alternative was for a train order that the crew could pick up "on the fly," without stopping; the agent informed the crew of this order by changing the signal from red to green twice. The third possibility was a train order that required the signatures of the crew; then the train had to stop, the orders were signed for, and the train was only then signaled to proceed.

"Originally, train orders were passed up on a bamboo hoop," Dick says, "then later, on a Y-shaped bracket on a pole beside the track. The order was attached to a loop of string clipped to the bracket; the fireman put his arm out of the cab of the locomotive and snagged the loop as they went by. Sometimes they missed, and then the train had to stop and he'd have to walk back to get the order."

The depot agent or the telegrapher on duty had a very strict routine to follow, particularly the standard operating procedures for the position of the signals. "When you had a train order to deliver you always kept your train order signal on red, indicating 'stop' to the train crew, unless the dispatcher had no order for the train and you had permission to clear the train through. But the engineer had to see the red signal first before you could clear it to green. Unless the office was closed, you always left the signal at red until you had eye contact with the train," Dick says.

Two big levers (one for each direction) on the operators table controlled the semaphore signal beside the depot. The big bay windows found in virtually all depots used for the train order control (TOC) system were designed to make it easy for the agent or telegrapher to look down the track without having to go outside.

But the agent or telegrapher's duty wasn't yet finished for this train movement. As the train passed the station, the telegrapher reported the event back to the dispatcher, with another message:

O S Algoma Train 625 by at 8:29 PM.

"O S" was understood to mean "on sheet," referring to the large sheet of paper used to chart the scheduled and actual progress of all the trains on the division during a twenty-four-hour period. This way the dispatcher could track the movement of the train, from waypoint to waypoint, and if necessary make adjustments with the train orders for all the trains using that section of track.

This old token turned up underneath the old 1864 depot at Santa Clara, three miles up the track from the San Jose depot where it belonged. Tokens exactly like this were provided to people checking parcels or baggage at depots all across the country a hundred years ago, just one of the many things every agent needed to know and take care of. *Ed Peterman collection*

As Dick Maurer recalls, "before you cleared a train you had to call the dispatcher and inform him of your intention, specifying the train order numbers. He gave you the OK and you recorded that in the clearance form, along with the chief dispatcher's initials."

Operator's Table

On the table in front of the bay window was the telegraph key and sounder, semaphore controls, and, later, a telephone set that was specially designed for the purpose of communicating with the dispatcher and other agents along the line. The mouthpiece was mounted on a pantograph and the earpiece was a headset, allowing the agent to use both hands to copy down train orders on the big upright typewriter in the middle of the table. Also on the table or within arm's reach was a cubbyhole with all the necessary

WILDERNESS

Previous page: When traffic became too busy for the agent to manage alone, some stations installed towers to control switches and signals.

Switches are controlled by these handles, each one controlling one of the many switches in the yard, in front of the station. The development of the "interlocking" switch in the 1880s was one of many major technological innovations that contributed to the development of railroads and the duties of the agent-telegrapher.

The switch controls and status board reveal the progress of train movement along one small segment of track. This is leading-edge technology, since replaced by the system trainmen call CTC—centralized traffic control.

Notes for the New Agent

This originally appeared in a wonderful little book about depots, long out of print, by Jim Bartz and "Bill" Williams; used here with permission.

The following is a memorandum from one small-town depot agent to his replacement, long ago, that offers some insights into the work of the agent and his or her relationship with the community of railroad employees and town residents.

As we will likely be very busy tomorrow transferring the accounts, I thought I would write down a few pointers to help you get your feet on the ground, things that might make your job a little easier in the next few weeks. You'll probably stub your toe a few times like I did, but maybe not as hard. Let me assure you that all of the railroad men working here, and all the folks in town, are absolutely first class, and will go more than half-way to become friends, and to help you get settled.

First of all, let me suggest that you print your name and date on the wall of the freight house, along with the rest of ours. It's sort of a club we have, and occasionally some old-timer will come by and go take a look at the names on the wall. It's nice to visit with them, if you aren't busy.

On account of no other housing being available in town, company living quarters is rent-free. They also furnish coal, and oil for the lamps. The water is good, and comes from the company water tank, at no charge to you. To prevent freezing of the pipes, keep all lines running a little when necessary.

The old clock on the wall is a good time-keeper, but has to be cocked slightly to the left for best results. There is a mark on the clock, and one on the wall, so keep the marks aligned. Some agents say that a clock needs fumes from a jigger of coal oil (placed inside the case) to keep it running properly, but this clock has always run just fine without it.

If you're looking for a place to eat, the house with its back yard bordering the right-of-way (over by the mail crane) has boarded telegraphers in the past. The lady can see the depot from the kitchen window, so when you "pull your boards in" to go to lunch, she will know to expect you in a few minutes. She'll have the meal on the table when you arrive. The regular boarding house in town is also open, and train crews eat there at times.

Hilna is the operator at the telephone company. She is a real nice girl, and she's always ready to "peddle old head" when she has the time. If you need to know where to locate someone to deliver a Western Union, some freight, or some express, she will be glad to help you.

The stove in the office is a good one. The way I have been doing it at night when I go off duty is to bank the fire and leave the stove door open. We have sheet metal on the floor, and I've never had any trouble with any coal popping out, which could risk burning the place down. For once we have a good grade of coal. Be sure you order plenty because sometimes it gets kind of chilly out here in the winter, down to 54 below at times. Also, we have quite a few hobos here, and I never get into trouble by starting a fire in the waiting room stove and letting them get warm.

According to the O.R.T. agreement, the company is to furnish wood in stove lengths for kindling. However, once they furnish the ties cut up into stove lengths we have to use the ax to split them up so we can use them for kindling. The section foreman knows this, so whenever you need any, let him know and be sure to let him know far enough ahead so that there will be no problem about it. They have a blanket authority to do that for us.

They don't have fire inspections too often here, but they do have them. It is kind of nice not to have to worry about them, so I have left the baggage room and freight house free of a lot of junk, and in the record room, things are picked up. When the auditor was here last time, he destroyed the old records which were beyond their retention periods. Fire inspectors will also check your company-owned living quarters.

Business has been good lately, so I have asked for a helper at the usual rate of $30 per month. If this is

approved, I hope you will consider Paul, the section foreman's son, as I promised him the job if I was still here.

The postmaster always has the mail sack ready thirty minutes before the train is due. In case you overlook hanging a sack, suggest you wire the mail clerk at the next stop, saying "no report." It has always been OK with the postmaster, and may save you the ten demerits I was awarded while learning that lesson.

Both eastbound and westbound trains "hit the bell" when they are about four miles out. Since either train would be coming up hill, you have about ten minutes before the train gets to the station. So when you tell the dispatcher that a train has just hit the bell, you still have some time to copy an order and get it fixed up in time.

The Trainmaster is a real fine man, and he is very neat and tidy. It's no secret that he likes to see the station clean. He is a promoted conductor and he has often spoken of how tidy he kept his caboose when he was a brakeman and I don't doubt it a bit. Now he won't attempt to interfere with your agency work unless he gets complaints. But there are two things he does know about: he knows what day it is, and he knows a clean floor when he sees one. It is his job to see if your train bulletin board is properly dated, and he'll check that for sure every time he comes around. Also, he expects you to have the station floor swept, and the station in a neat and orderly condition. Keeping the station clean will go a long way to avoid any small complaints from the Trainmaster.

To open the finger combination cash drawer, pull finger-holds number 1, number 2, and number 4, skipping number 3. The wooden tray has a hole worn into the penny compartment, but I became attached to it, so I have not asked for a replacement. The roll-top on the ticket case sticks a little, but the bridge and building gang is due soon to fix the stock pens, so you can ask the foreman to fix it without any red tape.

The lumber company has made it a policy of furnishing blocks of wood to the agent for his company living quarters, as well as the office. The company does supply coal for your office, as well as your living quarters, but if you prefer blocks, they will supply them for you. However, you are taking chances at having a car placed down at the mill and having the "local" bring it up to the depot. The Demurrage inspector can get mighty technical and can possibly assess you for a switching charge, but so far I have been able to get by without that.

The tariff inspector is about due. He comes around about every six months, so I've left the tariffs all filed and up to date. I think it is a good idea to keep them that way. If anything's not filed, and the inspector finds it missing, he will mail you another copy and you will have to file it anyway, so file all copies as soon as they arrive.

We have a couple of boys here in town who want to learn to telegraph. I've let them come in here and practice on the extra set I have here that belongs to the depot. Probably the kids (they are 13 or 14 years old) think that learning to telegraph only takes a few days, and chances are that they won't stick with it. But if it is convenient I wish you'd let them come around. They do get kind of a kick out of it, and if you're on the wire or on the dispatcher's phone, they know enough not to bother you. They are pretty good kids. They go get the mail for me quite often.

We use the manual block system on this end of the division, so you have a separate telegraph wire to the stations to the east and west. As you go home, be sure to put the plugs in the two lower hole in the plugboard to cut the wire through your board to the next station. This permits whichever stations are open to work together.

My sign is "V" and I'll be at station "BN" if you run into trouble. I realize that I probably forgot to answer a lot of questions you will have, so don't hesitate to get me on the wire.

Above: Don Douglas waves a salute to passing CalTrain 151 and gets a wave in reply. This tower at Santa Clara, California has been staffed around the clock for over half a century, sometimes by both Don and his wife. But the tower was retired shortly after this photograph was made in 1993, and the Douglases will soon be retired as well after many years as agents and telegraphers at stations on the Southern Pacific system.

Below: The old telephone isn't used much anymore; there's a radio on the table next to it to talk to the dispatcher or the train crews passing by. But one day, long ago, it was this quaint old antique that was the latest thing. It was a sad day for many agents when the telegraph keys and sounders were pulled from towers and depots in favor of the telephone, and many lamented the change.

forms for recording train orders, telegrams, clearance forms, and many other required documents.

Nearby would normally be two ink wells, one red and the other blue, with a tray for pens, fresh nibs, and pencils alongside or in a desk drawer. There was usually a brass seal and sealing wax for securing envelopes containing cash, a small sponge in a glass dish containing a bit of water (used to moisten the adhesive on envelopes), perhaps a brakeman's lantern and, most of the time, the agent's uniform cap.

The cap was a required item of apparel at train time, when the agent went out to help get baggage aboard and when meeting arriving passengers. In fact, the agent was expected to present a respectable appearance; for men, that meant stiff celluloid collars, ties, and clean white shirts. Women agents routinely wore long-sleeved blouses and long skirts, proper business attire back around the turn of the century.

At small, remote depots the agent would be responsible for all functions: keeping the place clean, paperwork filed, freight business attended to, tickets sold and cash accounted for, the outhouse cleaned

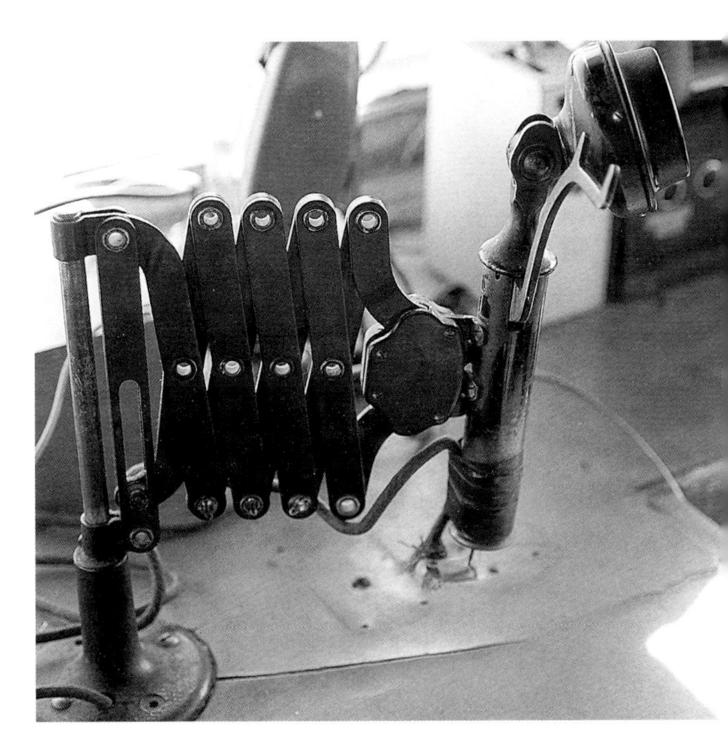

and limed, Western Union and Railway Express business managed, but most importantly, to record and pass along the train orders.

Henry Bender says, "When CTC was introduced, the railroads could close all those little depots, and they did. Southern Pacific gradually brought the whole system into CTC, from Salt Lake City to Oakland, but it took until the 1950s for the job to be completed."

Friend, Nebraska, is a lovely, friendly town that lived and died by the railroad. The depot has been repainted, and some of the commercial buildings still have a few tenants, although life in this small town has slowed nearly to a halt. But there are plans to use the depot again, perhaps as a police station, possibly as a museum.

CAFE

CHAPTER 2

A Short Course in Railroad Architecture

Developing an American Building

In the beginning, a railroad depot looked like any other public building. You could tell if you were near the depot because you found the railroad tracks. You purchased your ticket in a stage coach stop, a hotel, or the railway offices because all of these buildings served as early depot buildings.

It took about thirty years for America to evolve a building type that we now readily recognize as a railroad depot. It probably first appeared in a rural or suburban area where a new building to shelter passengers had to be built. But by the Civil War, in the 1860s, the single-story building that we know as a railroad depot had already developed most of its unique characteristics. And this profile remains so constant that we are still able to easily recognize a railroad depot in the landscape, even when it has been moved away from the tracks and modified as a residence, restaurant, or museum.

Its unique characteristics define it as a rectangular building with the longer side parallel to the railroad tracks. It is usually a single-story building without stairs or raised entryways, so that baggage and freight can be easily wheeled through the terminal to the trackside platform. The roof has a generous overhang to shelter passengers from the weather. A trackside bay window began to be a common feature in the 1870s, added to give agents better visibility along the tracks.

There was only one additional feature, usually added to the larger urban terminals starting about 1880, a clock tower. The railroad was responsible for introducing Standard

The San Carlos, California, depot was built from sandstone, hauled (by rail of course) from the Goodrich quarry in San Jose, about forty miles south. Contractors were using the same stone from the same quarry at the same time to build the nearby Stanford University campus. The original roof was supposed to be clay tile, but somehow the first roof was slate. This new roof is a replacement that was part of the recent restoration.

The railroads had standard designs for switches, milepost markers, crossing signs, station signs, roadbed section main and branch lines—all sorts of things were standardized, and depot designs were only one part of this. Standard designs were developed as early as 1863 on the San Francisco—San Jose line, and probably earlier in the East. They were "standard" only up to a point; a Southern Pacific Standard #23 might be 68 feet long, or it might be 78 feet, depending on the length of the freight room.

—*Henry Bender*

Time in the United States, developing the four time zones in 1883. Railroad depots began to feature clocks, partly to advertise railroad reliability and efficiency and partly to remind Americans that commerce moved to the tick of railroad time.

The shape of the depot building reflects the job it has to do... it's the old "form follows function" relationship. It took a few years for early railroaders to divide the labor of operating a railroad. By the time the various responsibilities were clearly sorted out, the depot had evolved to reflect the widely divergent functions. The passengers' waiting room was separated from the station agent's office. The railroad maintenance crews frequently maintained quarters well away from the depot.

Early depot restaurants were probably shared by passengers and train crews, but this practice quickly changed. What dainty passenger would want to occupy a chair recently vacated by a sooty, oil-soaked fireman? Separate facilities please!

Standard Designs

Standard depots were an extremely common type of building, especially as the a railroads were first laying track. The construction crews that were laying ties and spiking rail brought the first prefabricated depots along on one of the flatcars, the lumber having been precut at the mill. These depots were little more than shacks, designed to be temporary. Depots built along main lines or trunk lines were more substantial than lines that were just feeder railroads. But generally speaking, most of the first depots west of the Mississippi River were meant to be temporary buildings. Many were miles from any settlement and were only meant to serve railroad crews and agents.

Previous page: A few of the early depots were designed to appeal to vacationers. This one is near the Feather River Inn, California, and was intended to serve the new tourist passenger market that was made possible by the then-new rail network and the agressive fare competition between lines. *Library of Congress*

It would be difficult to describe this as a Victorian building since it appears to have discarded all of the fussy decorative detail we usually associate with Victorian architecture. Depot builders were already moving toward "American" forms of architecture. This is from Greenville, South Carolina, circa 1900. *Library of Congress*

As railroad traffic increased and towns developed, the depot buildings needed to be replaced. The size and type of the replacement depended on the amount of revenue the railroad was making in the community. Towns with a lot of bulky freight frequently warranted a separate freight building, instead of a "combination" depot; that is, one with the freight and passenger areas combined. By the 1870s most railroads had several "standard" depots in their contract files. They could quickly commission a local contractor or builder to erect a new depot if one should be lost by fire. (Frequently the fire had been started by the passing locomotive itself, the price of progress). And a standard building meant that construction costs could be estimated with certain reliability.

Railroad architects and construction engineers developed "standard" depots in basic designs that met the needs of most of the local communities. Standard depots such as Southern Pacific's No. 22 or No. 23 are actually second-generation depots, structures that replaced the first station structure that was probably just a shed at a flag stop. Standard depots began to be widespread replacements starting in the late 1870s, when more and more of the original depots were outgrown or destroyed by disaster. It is not always clear who should receive credit for some of the more unusual and interesting depot designs because plans only list the initials of the draftsman.

Who's Who in Depot Design—And What They Designed

E. Francis Baldwin

Baltimore & Ohio Station at Point of Rocks, Maryland. Fine Victorian Gothic building of brick construction, built by The Baltimore & Ohio Railroad. (Extant)

Solon Spencer Beman (1853-1914)

A Chicago architect and participant in the World's Colombian Exposition. Mr. Beman was chosen by railroad car magnate George Pullman to design his private home. Beman then designed the entire town of Pullman, a town of more than 1,800 structures for railroad car workers, the Pullman company offices, and several railroad terminal buildings. The most famous was probably the Grand Central Station in Chicago, built in 1890, since demolished.

Isaac C. Buckhout

With partner J.B. Snook he designed Grand Central Terminal, New York City (1869) for Commodore Vanderbilt.

Daniel Hudson Burnham (1846-1912)

Union Station, Washington, D.C., 1908. (Extant)

Graham Anderson Probst & White

Burnham successors. Union Station, Chicago, Illinois, 1926.

Bakewell & Brown

Santa Fe depot, San Diego, California, 1914. (Extant and recently restored-Amtrak)

Claude F. Bragdon (1866-1947)

The Terminal Station of the New York Central Railroad in Rochester, New York, seems to be his sole terminal structure. But he was an important writer and theorist whose ideas influenced other architects, both through his own essays and by publishing a series of books on architecture. Other terminal architects read his works.

A. Page Brown (1859-1896)

Southern Pacific Depot and the Ferry Building, San Francisco, California. Both were begun in 1893 and finished by Willis Polk in 1903 after Brown's accidental death.

Edward Burling (1819-1892)

Trained as a carpenter and contractor, he built many important commercial and civic buildings in Chicago and then was asked to rebuild them after the great Chicago fire. (His depot in Stillwater, Minnesota, was recently reproduced for a short line.)

Carrere, Hastings, Shreve and Lamb

Spanish Mission or colonial depot at Boise, Idaho, 1924.

L. Philips Clarke

West Palm Beach Passenger Station, 1925, for the Seaboard Air Line Railroad. (Extant)

Henry Ives Cobb (1859-1931)

Senior partner of Cobb & Frost, an early graduate of the architecture program at MIT, and participant at the Chicago World's Columbia Exposition. Chicago & Northwestern Railroad depots, in Waukesha, Wisconsin, and Milwaukee, Wisconsin; also a depot in Leavenworth, Kansas.

Cyrus Eidlitz

The Chicago & Western Indiana Terminal in Chicago and the Terminal Passenger Depot in Detroit, Michigan.

Fellheimer & Wagner

Cincinnati Union Terminal, Cincinnati, Ohio, 1933.

Frank Furness (1839-1912)

A Philadelphia native who built many depots for the Pennsylvania Railroad and made depots a specialty of his architectural practice. His projects for the Philadelphia & Reading Railroad include four station remodels, the Graver's Lane Station, Tabor Street, and Willing Alley. He designed a depot for Shamokin, reportedly unbuilt, but architectural drawings for this interesting building sometimes appear in reference collections.

For the Baltimore and Ohio Station he designed the Philadelphia Terminal on Chestnut Street and remodeled the Broad Street depot. He also built depots at Chester, Pittsburgh, Morrisville and Edgewood. He designed two depots for the B & O in Wilmington, Delaware, and an additional one in Frenchtown, Maryland.

Bradford Gilbert (1853-1911)

He was appointed architect to the New York, Lake Erie and Western Railroad in 1876 and designed a number of stations for that company. He remodeled the old Grand Central Station in New York City and built the Northern Pacific railway station in St. Paul, Minnesota. He also designed a depot in Sedalia, Missouri, now part of the Katy trail park system.

Jarvis Hunt (1859-1941)

Union Station, Kansas City, Missouri (Extant—Amtrak), as well as railroad terminals in Dallas, Texas, and Joliet, Illinois. A nephew of prominent Beaux Arts architect Richard Morris Hunt, Jarvis Hunt was trained at Harvard and at the new architecture school at Massachusetts Institute of Technology.

J.D. Isaacs and D.J. Patterson

Southern Pacific Depot, San Antonio, Texas 1902, and Tucson, Arizona.

J. F. Kemp

Camden Street Station, Baltimore & Ohio Railroad, 1852.

F. H. Kimball

Reading Terminal, Philadelphia, Pennsylvania.

Benjamin Henry Latrobe II

The son of the famous architect; Relay Station, Relay, Maryland, 1870s.

B.F. Levet

San Juan Capistrano, AT&SF depot, 1894.

Theodore C. Link and Edward B. Cameron

Union Station, St. Louis, Missouri, 1892. (Extant—Amtrak Access)

Mathison & Howard

Southern Pacific Depot, Burlingame, California, 1893. Reported to be the oldest extant depot in the Mission style in America.

Philip Thornton Mayre

Atlanta, Georgia, depot in the grand Spanish style, 1905.

Mead, McKim & White

The famous and now vanished Pennsylvania Station in New York, New York, built in 1910, demolished 1966.

Richard Montfort

Union Station, Nashville, Tennessee, 1900, a Richardsonian Romanesque with an impressive clock tower. (Extant—Amtrak)

Harvey L. Page

International & Great Northern Depot, San Antonio, Texas, 1907.

John (1861-1935) and Donald (1895-1945) Parkinson

A father and son, both architects, from Los Angeles, California. They designed the Arcade Passenger Depot of the Southern Pacific Railroad in Los Angeles, and the Los Angeles Union Terminal Buildings, Los Angeles, California, during the early 1930s. In addition, they designed a number of large terminals across the western states, including the second Union Railroad Terminal at Ogden, Utah, and the Union Railroad Terminal in Salt Lake City, Utah. Their depot and division office at Caliente, Nevada, is currently undergoing restoration. An identical mission revival depot at Milford, Utah, and a similar structure at Kelso, California, are also credited to the Parkinsons.

D. J. Patterson

Union Pacific Passenger Depot, Salt Lake City, Utah. Patterson was a Union Pacific engineer. The terminal was rebuilt in 1909, combining the Second Empire and Beaux Arts styles.

Peabody, Sterns and Ferber

Duluth, Minnesota, terminal, 1892, which is quite similar to the St. Louis Union Station. Now renovated and recycled for use as a cultural center.

Willis Polk

Western Pacific Depot, Sacramento, California, 1910. (Extant—Amtrak) A brilliant designer, historian Harold Kirker calls him the *enfant terrible* of western architecture.

John Russell Pope (1834-1937)

Union Station, Richmond, Virginia, 1926.

Reed & Stem

With Warren & Wetmore, they designed the Grand Central Station in New York City, 1913.

Charles Reed (1857-1911)

Partner in Reed and Stem, designed more than 100 railroad stations, including the Grand Central Station Terminal in New York City.

Henry Hobson Richardson (1838-1886)

Five depots for the Boston and Albany Railroad, including Auburndale, Massachusetts (1881), Palmer, Massachusetts (1881), Framingham, Massachusetts (1883), Wellesley, Massachusetts (1884), and North Easton, Massachusetts (1886). Developed the "commuter" depot in and around the Boston area. Noted for his distinctive use of Romanesque forms, his style became widely (and sometimes badly) imitated for depots and other public buildings.

Thomas Rodd

Union Station, Indianapolis, Indiana, 1886-1889.

Spier & Rohns

Grand Trunk Depot, Battle Creek Michigan, 1906.

Allen H. Stem (1856-1931)

Partner in Reed and Stem, designed more than 100 railroad stations including the Grand Central Station Terminal in New York City.

Benjamin Bosworth Smith

Union Station, Montgomery, Alabama, 1897, an impressive Victorian Gothic style terminal.

Gilbert Stanley Underwood

Marysville, Kansas, and Cozad, Nebraska.

Henry Van Brunt (1832-1903)

A partner in Ware & Van Brunt, and Van Brunt & Howe. In 1881 partner William Ware was appointed head of the new architecture department at Massachusetts Institute of Technology in Boston, leaving Van Brunt to form a new partnership with Frank Howe. Van Brunt closed his Boston office in 1886 and opened a new office in Kansas City, Missouri. He designed a number of Union Pacific railroad stations between Sioux City, Iowa, and Portland, Oregon, Stations along the Union Pacific Line because of his friendship with railroad company president Charles Francis Adams. They included Union Station in Cheyenne, Wyoming, the Union Station in Sioux City, Iowa, a Union Station for Portland, Oregon, and a depot in Lawrence, Kansas. He was a participating architect for the World's Colombian Exhibition, held in Chicago in 1893.

Warren & Wetmore

Worked with Reed and Stem.

Charles Whittlesey

Santa Fe architect.

Joseph M. Wilson

Designed the depot in Washington, D.C., for the Pennsylvania Railroad; also designed the first Broad Street Station in Philadelphia, which was later remodeled by Frank Furness.

H. Wolters

Union Station, Louisville, Kentucky, 1882.

The MoPac depot at Jefferson City, Missouri, combines creamy Missouri limestone with dark red brick for stunning effect.

Defining the Style

Up until the Civil War, the prevailing architectural styles used for most American public buildings were copied from ancient Roman temples or medieval European cathedrals. Early depot buildings tended to be utilitarian train sheds, although some graceful and charming depots were built in major cities. The Mount Clare depot in Baltimore survives as the oldest depot building in America. It is thoughtfully designed, a handsome brick structure, octagonal in shape, designed as the office of the fledgling Baltimore & Ohio Railroad.

Colonial America looked to England for depot design inspiration. The English railroad stations of the 1830s had demonstrated that the special design problems posed by trains could be sensibly resolved. Engineering, planning, and aesthetics could be successfully combined. Early depots sometimes spanned two tracks and were designed to protect passengers on one or two trains from bad weather. But the demand for service quickly outgrew a single shed, and depot builders quickly adapted European style terminals which could accommodate several trains.

Depots were designed to fit into the existing cities, and in most old downtowns, space was frequently limited. Sometimes depots were added to hotels or stage stops without any consideration for safety. Rails were laid along the existing turnpike or canal paths. There was little reason to develop a special sort of building to serve just the railroad, although it was becoming apparent to railroad operators and passengers alike that the existing depots were pretty uncomfortable.

The heyday of depot and terminal construction, from the 1880s until the beginning of the 1929 Depression, coincides with the development of an American architectural style. Today we can easily look at a building and say "that looks French" or "that reminds me of a Swiss chalet." But back in 1900 it was nearly impossible to look at buildings and identify them as typically and authentically American. American archi-

The Cheyenne, Wyoming, depot exterior construction was red and gray sandstone, carefully fitted and elaborately carved.

The depot is in Cheyenne, Wyoming, but the building stone was especially quarried and shipped from Colorado. The architectural style is called Romanesque; the massive arches with the carefully shaped keystone are important characteristics of the style.

Nevada used to have several combination depots like this Southern Pacific Standard No. 23, which is still beside the tracks in Lovelock. This is one of the few remaining such depots in the Silver State and it is rather neglected and unloved, despite the attempts of some in the community to put life back in the building. The "Standard Combination" name comes from its having the freight office at one end and the passenger waiting room at the other, while the agent lived upstairs.

This bracket detail from the eaves of the Lovelock, Nevada, depot demonstrates the workmanship of some of the Southern Pacific carpenter shops. Although the Standard Combination depots were just that... standard, some carpenters managed to dress them up with some special detailing.

tects were experimenting with designs that could truly be identified as "American", styles that were somehow an expression of our values and ideals.

We see exciting design experiments during the 1880s and 1890s as American architects discovered the building forms of the Spanish explorers and missionaries and the native Americans in the Southwest. The Atchison, Topeka & Santa Fe was the first railroad to experiment with an American design idiom. Other railroads followed, to a lesser degree, adapting designs to the local weather and social conditions. For example, the open air depots along the Florida coast combine the Spanish architectural design elements with the open verandahs desirable in hot muggy climates. The Spanish or "mission style depot in chillier Boonville, Missouri, is enclosed.

Henry Hobson Richardson and Depot Romanesque

In the very recent past, railroad architecture seemed to be classified into only two categories. The first was for structures designed by Henry Hobson Richardson and his imitators; the second category included everything else. Richardson designed a great number of railroad depots as well as other public buildings. His unique style became so popular that today we call it "Richardsonian Romanesque." Depots with the characteristic Richardsonian style stonework appear in such far-flung locations as San Carlos, California, and Shawnee, Oklahoma.

Why was the work of this Boston architect so popular? And how did this particular style become to be so widespread and so widely associated with railroad depots? The best answer seems to be that

Brigham City, Utah, still has a very active depot although it no longer serves passengers. This handsome building still serves as a crew office for the railroad, and is still largely intact, inside and out.

The Amtrak stops at Lee's Summit, Missouri, but not at this depot. This little building has been polished, but passengers are sheltered at an "Amshack" on the other side of the tracks. Note the mileage signs telling travelers how close—or far—they are from the next big cities, Kansas City and St. Louis.

Previous page: Glenwood Springs, Colorado, has a depot built by the Denver and Rio Grande. Amtrak stops here for you summer and winter if you like Rocky Mountain scenery, clean air and soaking at the hot springs. Glenwood Springs was an important resort before the railroad ever came to town. The Native Americans first discovered the springs in the area; now it's a popular retreat for many vacationers.

You can bring your skis to the depot in Glenwood Springs, Colorado. This Rocky Mountain depot is prepared for winter visitors; the freight room has extra space for weekend skiers from nearby Denver.

Richardson, a talented and personable individual, was in the right place at the right time.

Born in New Orleans, Henry Hobson Richardson attended architecture school at Beaux Arts in France. He left America to study abroad in 1859 at age twenty, just before the Civil War began. In a fortunate sequence of circumstances, he found work as an architectural draftsman in France after graduation, apprenticing with an architect who was specializing in railroad depots. Railroad design and development in Europe was already a decade ahead of America railway construction. And the Civil War was delaying American railroad development even more.

When Richardson returned to America in 1866, just after the war ended, his service was in great demand. There was a great deal of rebuilding that needed to be done after the war, and very few trained architects. And an architect with actual railroad engineering training and construction experience was especially

The Durand, Michigan, depot was completed in 1905 to serve the Grand Trunk Railroad. Built at the juncture of several railroad lines, Durand was reportedly the second busiest depot in Michigan. Detroit was the busiest. *Robert Genat*

rare. He settled in the Boston area and soon had a very substantial design practice.

Richardson was very talented but also in very poor health during the peak of his creativity. He suffered from nephritis, Bright's disease, a kidney ailment that pushed his weight up to nearly 350 pounds and made it difficult for him travel. It was a disease which ended his remarkable career at age forty-eight, an age when most architects are just beginning to be most prolific. He worked around his physical limitations, delegating much of the work to his assistants. Working from home, he hired the best and most talented architects he could find to work with him. The new architecture department at nearby Massachusetts Institute of Technology and his Beaux Arts associates provided Richardson with many productive assistants and draftsmen, including Shepley, Rutan and

The round tower on the upstairs corner of the Durand, Michigan, depot gave the traffic supervisor a good view in all directions. *Robert Genat*

Bottom left: Even the doorknobs are special in the depot building at Durand, Michigan. *Robert Genat*

Bottom right: Depot design anticipated large numbers of people meeting trains at all hours, winter and summer, under blazing sunshine and winter snows, and tried to provide reasonable protection from the elements. Passengers waited under the eaves for their trains in Durand, Michigan. *Robert Genat*

This handsome little depot at Grass Lake, Michigan, is in excellent condition, thanks to the energetic efforts of the community it once served. Like so many other depots across the US, this structure doesn't really fit into the late 20th Century but is far too important and attractive to discard. Community supporters who made contributions to its restoration have their names on the bricks around the depot. *Robert Genat*

Pressed tin was a commonly used roofing material at the turn of the century; this example photographed in Nebraska features an uncommon pattern.

Decorative detailing was provided by an especially talented brickmason for the Huron, South Dakota, depot.

Coolidge, the architects who would eventually take over much of Richardson's work.

Railroad Architects

In the beginning, large depots in major cities were designed by architectural firms who were experienced in designing large public buildings. Small depots were built by the same railroad construction contractors who were laying rail and building maintenance sheds. As railroads became more prosperous, many of them hired an architect for their engineering staff, someone who understood the special design requirements imposed by railroad safety.

Railroad terminal architects seemed to be a small fraternity. Many received architectural training at the Ecole des Beaux Arts in Paris and had the opportunity to participate in the Chicago World's Columbia Exposition in 1893. Many of them were associated with the new architecture and railroad engineering programs which were just getting underway at Massachusetts Institute of Technology in Boston. And they were all

A unique Union Pacific logo was formed in custom-cast architectural terra-cotta for the exterior detailing of the depot at Marysville, Kansas. Gilbert Stanley Underwood was the architect for this depot, which today is still a very active crew change office.

practicing design at a time we now recognize as the "Golden Age of Railroad Building," the years from 1890 to about 1915.

What Style Is That Depot?

What is "style" and why is it important? In depot design, style is the effort a railroad company made to make their railroad unique. Sometimes it was using a characteristic color to identify their depots and rolling stock, sometimes it was a special company logo such as the Santa Fe cross on the ends of all the depots.

We pay a lot of attention to building style because it is a very important clue to a depot's age and construction. Style tells us a lot about the pocketbooks and social values of the railroad company that first built the depot. There are several architectural style guidebooks available, probably the best being "What Style Is It," available from the National Trust for Historic Preservation. Analyzing depot styles can be confusing, especially when the architect has combined two or three of his favorites. So here are a few style terms that you will find frequently used to describe depots and terminals.

A quick note here. Shops and roundhouses were not built in a "style". They were built to be strictly utilitarian. However, they are very important to American architectural history because of their straightforward design, craftsmanship, and scarcity.

So you will frequently see detailed architectural descriptions of these structures because the few remaining examples are so varied and so unique.

'Amshack'

Rhymes with Amtrak, a very spare modular structure without grace, charm, or decorative detail. Built after 1970, these Spartan structures were built by Amtrak to serve as passenger shelters all along the railroad lines. An Amshack can frequently be found on or near the platform of an abandoned depot.

There are those who feel the stark designs could possibly be classified under the International style; others think that International style architects Philip Johnson and Louis Kahn would be profoundly insulted.

Beaux Arts

A very decorative style of depot building, usually found in larger depots in major cities. Popular around the 1900s, this term is usually applied to monumental depots of colossal scale. It became popular after the World's Colombian Exposition, held in Chicago in1893. Many of the architects who designed a Beaux Arts structure for this Expo also designed a major railroad depot or two. And since many major metropolitan depots were built around the turn of the century, they were built in the most popular style of the time... Beaux Arts. The style combines enormous arches, domes, colonnades, and columns in dramatic and sometimes pompous manner. Named for the French School of Design, formally known as Nationale Ecole des Beaux Arts (National School of Fine Art), many major urban terminals were designed by American architects who had attended this important school. It takes an extraordinary designer to lavish decorative detail on a structure with elan', n'est pas?

Chateau

Depots and terminals went through a period of looking like French castles and estates, due in large part to the extraordinary popularity of the design of the St. Louis Union Terminal in 1894. This was also a popular style in Canada, especially in the areas of the country with a cultural influence from the early French colonies. These depots frequently feature dressed stone exteriors with decorative ironwork on top of their deeply sloped roofs.

Colonial

(Early 19th century) The man on the street calls it "colonial" if it has columns and looks like Monticello.

Previous page: Architectural terra-cotta details outline the entryways at the Union Pacific depot in Marysville, Kansas.

A Victorian-era cast iron column detail from the platform of a rural Nebraska depot.

Architectural historians see "colonial" as a type of structure built before 1800, usually resembling the salt box cottages of Massachusetts and Connecticut. It is not a style that appears in municipal buildings.

Depots with columns and domes, the ones that do look like Mount Vernon or Monticello, are classified as either Greek revival or Roman revival. Architects were attempting to imitate Greek and Roman temples because it was felt that the ancients had successfully defined perfection in philosophy and design.

Craftsman

This is a 20th century style, frequently seen in suburban depots built after 1900. The Kirkwood, Missouri, depot is a good example of the style, so is the Green River, Wyoming, depot. Style characteristics include shingles and blackened brick known as clinker brick for exterior surfaces. Interiors frequently feature open-beamed ceilings. The style developed as a direct reaction to the fussy, overly decorated Victorian styles.

Edwardian

(Early 20th century) This term is sometimes applied to structures built just after Queen Victoria died and her son Edward succeeded her on the throne. The Edwardian era spans 1902 to about 1912. American depot architects were building mission revival or craftsman style depots during this time.

Gothic

From the Goths (otherwise known as the French if you are not speaking Latin), a building style used in the medieval cathedrals. Style characteristics include pointed arches, steeples, and pointed roofs. Americans and Europeans imitated this style in the nineteenth century, using wood rather than the stone that the cathedral builders had used. It is referred to as Gothic Revival and it was all the rage for furniture, fences, and decorative detailing as well as house design.

We refer to this style as "carpenter Gothic," and it was widely used across America to showcase the skill and ingenuity of local carpenters and builders. Few early carpenters had access to a lathe to manufacture elaborate turnings, so many of these early depots are extraordinary gems of craftsmanship and inventiveness.

Greek Revival

In depot design, this means that the architect decorated his structure with columns. Depots were supposed to look impressive and demonstrate something about local community values to the visitor. For decades, the best way to impress the public, architecturally speaking, was to imitate the Parthenon. It showed awareness of the importance of Greek antiquities, an appreciation for the philosophic and intellectual contributions of the Greeks to the Western world. It was a very long reach. Nevertheless, it was an extremely important statement for a small town that might otherwise be seen as a cultural backwater when compared to other towns up and down the railroad.

"The Harriman's"

Edward Harriman became director of the failing Union Pacific about 1897 and restored it to financial health. With its profits he acquired a major share of the Southern Pacific and then the ownership of the Central Pacific railroads. Decrepit depots were replaced during his tenure and all three lines saw major capital improvements in trackage, facilities, and rolling stock.

Many depots were forty years old by this time. Harriman replaced them with "standard" depots. Construction plans for these depots commonly appear in plan books for railroad modelers as the Southern Pacific 23 or 24. They are also sometimes known as "The Harriman's."

AD
1893

Italianate

Depots in the Italianate style appear before the Civil War, about the mid-1840s and again forty years later when the Victorians revived the style... again. Depots built in the 1840s in the early Italianate style are probably all demolished, although we still have many excellent photographic examples. Depots built in the Victorian Italianate style of the 1880s are more common. An identifying characteristic is the detailing at the corners of the buildings. Called "quoins," these additions are meant to imitate stone structures found in Italy.

Mission and Mission Revival

The California missions were built by Franciscan missionaries from 1769 to about 1823. Technically, there were "missions" built throughout the American Southwest and into Mexico and Central America during this era, but the specific mission buildings that influenced American depot architecture were concentrated in California along El Camino Real.

"Mission" architectural style should correctly be called "Mission Revival", but historians usually refer to it as simply as "mission." Sometimes it is also loosely referred to as "Spanish style" or "California" style, but the building characteristics are similar.

A Mission style depot is identified as a stucco, plaster, or adobe building, frequently with a roof made of curved tiles. Additional embellishments sometimes include a decorative quatrefoil window, glazed ceramic tiles, and a covered colonnade which serves as an open porch. The more elaborate depots also added a bell tower, sometimes with a decorative bell.

Moderne

After 1925, a new style of design from Europe had a profound affect on all industrial design, including railroads. We frequently refer to it as "aerodynamic" or "streamlined." It changed the shape of our automobiles, airplanes, and, of course, our locomotives and depots. The name comes from the Exposition Internationale des Artes Decoratifs et Industriels Moderne, held in Paris in 1925. We sometimes also refer to it as Art Deco, another name derived from the same Exposition.

Queen Anne

This is one of the building styles popular around 1880, usually seen in larger houses but sometimes seen in public buildings such as depots. Unlike Victorian, Edwardian, and Tudor, the name Queen Anne has nothing to do with styles borrowed from structures built during the reign of an English queen. It's just a name.

The style features a round tower, or half-tower, usually built into the corner of the depot, with a pointed roof that looks like a witch's hat. There is usually a lot of decorative detail, scrolls, and curlicues, generously lavished under the eaves around the windows and railings. Shingles on the sides and roofs are arranged in decorative patterns, and porch rails are elaborately turned and decorated.

Revival

This is a very loose term; most depot styles are revivals from another period. However... sometimes you will see a depot that is referred to as "original" or "eclectic." This either means that it is the work of a genius who designed something truly unique, or it is the work of someone who mixed so many styles that the structure is impossible to describe.

Romanesque

The ancient Romans developed the dome and the arch to create stone bridges and open airy public buildings. Historians commonly acknowledge these important engineering developments by using the name "Romanesque" to refer to arches worked in heavy stone with a "keystone" at the top of the arch. Cathedral builders turned to "Roman" architecture during the Middle Ages, using the dome and arch to construct cathedrals and castles.

And nineteenth century architects again looked for inspiration in the classic forms, reviving the medieval Romanesque designs and building depots in a style we now refer to as "Romanesque revival." Depot architect H.H. Richardson used this style so much that he is credited with an American building style now known as Richardsonian Romanesque.

Second Empire

The Empire they are referring to is French, and the style was introduced to America around 1870, when Paris was being rebuilt. This style was extremely popular on the East Coast and many public buildings in Washington, D.C., were built in the Second Empire style. Style characteristics include a mansard roof, tiny windows in the attic, and lacy iron grillwork. The Bethlehem, Pennsylvania, depot built in 1873 is a good example. Today we tend to identify this as just another fussy Victorian style; we are unable to distinguish its unique characteristics. Only the mansard roof line remains as a clue.

It's a magnificent French chateau built in 1892 but it appears in midwestern St. Louis, Missouri. Construction of the St. Louis Union Station set off a trend for chateau-style depots across the country.

The St. Louis, Missouri, Union Station features lacy cast iron grill work in these supports for the building's eaves at the main entrance. It seems that wherever possible on this station, surfaces and structures were made as ornate as possible.

No expense was spared in materials or design for the St. Louis Union Station. They wanted something that would hold up for decades, and this building has lasted more than a century.

Stick Style and Eastlake

Popular from about 1870 to 1885, this refers to designs for homes and public buildings with decorative detail applied directly to the facades. Stick-style is plainer, using just flat boards, sometimes in crisscrosses for decoration. Eastlake uses boards cut and pierced with a bandsaw, and every inch of the exterior is covered with some sort of ornamental embellishment.

An English designer, Charles Locke Eastlake, was a critic of the overly fussy Gothic Revival decor of the late 1860s. He promoted clean and simple lines in interior furnishings and architecture. To his horror he found his name somehow associated with some of the most detailed and elaborate furnishings and building styles imaginable.

Tudor

This is another revival style; you, of course, were not misled because you recognize immediately that railroads appeared centuries later than the 16th century Tudor kings of England. Tudor style depots look like English inns and manor houses. They are frequently brick or stone with half-timbering on the upper walls and slate roofs. Tudor revival styles in depot design seem to reappear periodically. There were quite a few built in this style in the late 1920s, when Tudor

It's called the whispering hall because the acoustics allow conversations at one end of the room to be overheard at the other end. The magnificent frescoes were designed by a local firm in the St. Louis Union Station.

was revived, again! Examples are found particularly in northeastern areas.

This is a very popular style of depot east of the Mississippi River, where brick, stone, and slate are common building materials. Tudor revival and half-timbered styles have always been popular in England, where many depot structures have used these design elements for centuries. Once again, the colonies—America and Canada—borrow depot design ideas from Europe.

Vernacular

A term usually applied to a depot structure that was built by local carpenters; a structure that does not imitate a named style. Vernacular depot structures are extremely rare and therefore extremely valuable. They are usually tiny, built of local materials by local craftsmen and date from the earliest railroad building along that line. A vernacular depot could be a log cabin, and a few depots really are. But to be considered vernacular log cabins, they would have to date from a time when a log cabin was the only sort of shelter available. Vernacular buildings are extremely vulnerable to those architectural ignoramuses who think a depot has to look fancy to be important. Washington, Missouri, or Florrisant, Missouri are vernacular depots; very early simple buildings by local carpenters.

MENLO PARK
MENLO PARK
CHAMBER
OF
COMMERCE

Victorian

A Victorian building is one that was built when Queen Victoria of England was on the throne. She ruled from 1837 to 1901, the era that covers most of the glorious age of railroad construction. Since her reign spanned such a long period, most architectural historians subdivide it. The Gothic Revival depot styles appear as an early Victorian style around the 1850s; the Romanesque, Eastlake, and Stick styles appear later, after 1880. Queen Anne is also a late Victorian style.

By the end of Victoria's reign, a distinctly American style of building was beginning to emerge. American architects were experimenting and developing new styles to express America's values and attitudes.

Previous page: Menlo Park, California, was originally a plain little depot in 1865; just a square shed. But it needed some suitable trim when students entering nearby Stanford University started detraining here. The bay window and Victorian gingerbread were added in the 1880s and the depot recently received a major renovation.

It's a Richardsonian depot way out west in San Carlos, California. Built around 1888, this depot was apparently designed by the firm of Shepley, Rutan and Coolidge. They were just down the road working on the Stanford University campus for railroad magnate Leland Stanford.

WAUSEON

Depot Architecture

What Makes Some Styles 'Good'?

Why do the so-called experts rave about depots that look like a dirty, decrepit pile of bricks? What makes some depots really wonderful and especially worth saving? What are the yardsticks that these experts are using? Here are a few of the basic ideas.

Architects and architectural historians usually say that a building must possess a threefold combination of usefulness, engineering, and beauty to be considered wonderful. All good buildings have to pass these basic measures. Architects frequently use an expression coined by Sir Henry Wotten, "commodity, firmness, delight." These guidelines apply to old buildings as well as new ones. So let's apply these three measures to depots.

Commodity

A successful depot building has to accommodate a number of conflicting functions within the building. It has to serve large groups of people on one side of the building, at the same time providing office space for railroad personnel. Since all of those passengers can interfere with the safe operation of an arriving train, the waiting room needs to comfortably accommodate the travelers until the traffic operations manager allows passengers to board.

A depot serves an extremely important railroad network traffic function, maintaining schedules and keeping trains from colliding. Staff members need to be able to concentrate on rail traffic flow without unnecessary inter-

Waseon is a great place to sit and watch the trains go by, and folks still make a special trip to Waseon, Ohio, to check the traffic. This depot is as American as its location, a solid, functional but graceful structure that has served its community for decades.

When Southern Pacific built Ogden's Union Station, their architects included some charming little details like the mosaic tile work over the doors and the wrought iron light fixtures. Both are strictly decorative elements that added extra cost but helped make a building that was, among other things, a temple to the machine age.

ruptions. A depot is frequently a freight shipment point, handling tons of freight, some of it fragile and perishable, all of it valuable.

Track maintenance crews received information from the depot office about road conditions. This crew would never appear in the public waiting rooms of large depots, but they still needed an office or area to pick up their maintenance orders and punch a time-clock. Frequently these laborers are (or at least they were) so scruffy that their activities were are relegated to an entirely separate building at the station, but their work is critical in bad weather.

A depot was a 24-hour a day building... for engineers, for telegraphers, for railroad crews, and for passengers. Trains can run late, so passengers sometimes have to wait hours for connections, trying to pass time comfortably while still keeping a watchful eye, or ear, on arrival announcements. So while the big restaurants in the depot were are closed at night, there was frequently a coffee shop where passengers and railroad crews, hack drivers, and telegraphers could can wait with some degree of comfort.

Railroad travel bundles all sorts of people together in one space; people who would frequently prefer not to be introduced and who would not want know each other socially. So depots became a curious sort of public/private space. It was not a public building in the same way a courthouse, city hall, or school was public. And it was a building that was clearly in private ownership. But you could go

Kansas City's Union Station was designed for a community of two million people at a time when the city included only a tenth of that population. It was an overly generous building throughout its life, but was the showplace of the city even so. The heating bill for its last months of operation in the 1970s was $80,000.

Here's a stock certificate for the capital stock of the Yazoo and Mississippi Valley Railroad Company, as issued in New York City. This certificate is a cherished artifact of the small railroad. In some cases, the only remnants of such a rail company are its small depots, and they, too, are beloved by rail fans. While the certificate depicted a clipper on the right, there was a nice woodcut of a depot scene at the center of the sheet.

freely to a depot, 24 hours a day, and as long as you didn't get in the way, your presence was tolerated.

A depot was a good meeting place. It was easy to find. You just followed the tracks or listened for the whistle. So if you said, "Meet me in front of the depot," a person who was totally unfamiliar with the town could easily find you, have a cup of coffee in the coffee shop, conduct business, and then travel on. In a small town, of course, there was no privacy since the station agent knew everyone in town. On the other hand, if you were looking for someone in a small town, you could just drop by the station and ask the agent.

Inside the depot various groups of people had to be managed; on the street outside the depot, vehicles had to be managed. There was a lot of meeting and greeting that took place at a depot, passengers and baggage, departing and arriving. There was a lot of bustle; hacks, pedestrians, autos, wagons, buses. Most passengers focused only on their own baggage and their own destination. A good depot provided a safe and comfortable area for arriving and departing travelers, and all of the transport that serves them.

Commodity is a yardstick that should still be used when evaluating aging depots for reuse. The Kansas City Union Station was originally built before escalators. Passengers had difficulty finding a porter willing to haul heavy baggage from trackside up to the hack stand at the front entrance. Some depots still manage to serve passengers and staff with comfort, and some never could.

A depot building has to manage all of these competing requirements with efficiency. It had to have enough room for passengers, but not too much. A really first-class terminal had accommodations for the arrival of a President or a Queen. It had to provide a high level of service, 24 hours a day. These are all tests of "commodity."

Firmness

Depots present special engineering design problems that are unique to the nature of railways. First, a locomotive is a large, dangerous, dirty, and mobile piece of equipment. Steam en-

Twenty years of deferred maintenance at the Kansas City Union Station, in Kansas City, Missouri, have resulted in rusted out portions of the pressed steel and cast iron canopy. The detail, particularly right at the corner of the canopy, is exquisite.

Economic Events in America That Affected Railroad Depot Construction

Depots, roundhouses, and terminals cost money, lots of it, and depot construction was affected by the highs and lows of the American economy.

1830 Railroads carrying passengers appear on the east coast. On August 25, a 13-mile trial trip from Baltimore to Ellicott City is made. And on December 25, the Best Friend of Charleston inaugurates regular passenger service 136 miles from the port of Charleston, South Carolina to Hamburg, S.C.

Today the Mount Clare Station in Baltimore, MD is considered to be the oldest surviving depot structure. It is used as a railroad museum by the Baltimore & Ohio Railroad.

Railroad construction and development are financed by both American and European interests.

1848 First direct mail route on railroad completed.

1849 Gold is discovered in California. It brings in wealth, but construction dollars are invested in mining equipment rather than railroads.

1851 First recorded use of the telegraph for train dispatch.

1855 The Sacramento to Folsom railroad opens, primarily to haul mining equipment from the port of Sacramento to the Gold Country.

1859 Silver is discovered in Nevada, the Comstock Lode rush begins. Short line railroad construction is underway to haul the ore and ingots.

1860 Chicago now has eleven railroads and is the leading railroad hub in America.

1861 The Civil War begins. Railroads bring men and material to the battlefronts and new railroad construction supports the war efforts in the North and South.

Prices for iron for rails and rolling stock rises. Civilian railroad building halts.

1864 January 14, The San Francisco to San Jose railroad opens, 49 miles linking San Jose and San Francisco.

1865 The Civil War is over and railroad rebuilding begins.

New depots are built throughout the South to replace buildings lost in the war.

The race for the great intercontinental railroad begins and small depots, many of them temporary are built along the line.

1869 The Golden Spike links the inter-continental railroad on May 10. Instead of bringing wealth to California from expanded markets in the East, it brought increased competition and an economic depression. The railroad runs both ways, as the old saying goes.

1873 Another silver bonanza discovered in the Comstock in Nevada.

1876 Date approximate, Fred Harvey opens a restaurant at a Santa Fe depot in Topeka, Kansas.

1877 Telephone communications for railroad use first tested.

1880s Railroad competition and depot expansion. Competing lines each built depots; some small towns end up with four and five depots. Likewise major cities find themselves with several Union Terminals, more than the local economy can support.

1883 Railroads adopt Standard time, a four time-zone system developed by the railroad and in general use by the rest of the country. Congress finally made it official in 1918. Clock towers become an important feature in depot construction.

1893 A serious national depression sets in, brought on by railroad competition and speculation.

1890s Railroad consolidations bring efficiencies.

1900s Radical changes in technology, the widespread use of electricity, especially in urban centers affects train operation and depot construction. Most depots are now old and obsolete. A new wave of depot construction begins, replacements for old depots.

1917 America enters the first World War. Railroads are nationalized and many depots are modified by the government to support wartime activities. Routine maintenance suffers.

1920 Another decade of depot and terminal construction begins as American prosperity spreads.

1924 Approximate peak of railroad passenger traffic. Except for the exceptional traffic during wartime, this is the peak for passenger service.

1925 First diesel locomotive introduced in switching service.

1928 Railway Express Agency formed.

1929 The stock market crashes and The Depression begins. Some depots and terminals are built but for the most part these are buildings that were designed and planned before 1929.

The Depression 30s Several extraordinary Grand Union Terminals appear, including Cincinnati in 1933 and Los Angeles.

Other depots appear, but these are sponsored as WPA projects, construction projects for public buildings sponsored by the federal government to provide employment in these hard times.

1941 First diesel freight locomotives placed in regular service.

1939 to 1945 America enters World War II in 1941. The railroads are nationalized again. Major terminals experience enormous passenger traffic from military personnel going to training camps. St. Louis Terminal sees 100,000 passengers a day in 1943; and New York's Pennsylvania Station collects nearly 179,000 tickets on Christmas eve on 1943.

1950 to present Depot replacement only; new depots are small and Spartan.

1974 AMTRAK created by Congress to salvage and protect the remaining passenger rail lines in America. Depot construction limited to tiny passenger shelters known as Amshacks.

1977 The Ogden Union Station reopens.

1985 The St. Louis Union Station reopens.

1993 The Washington, D.C. Union Station reopens.

1993 The Emeryville Depot appears.

An entryway at the Kansas City Union Station, Kansas City, Missouri. The elements are beginning to erode some of the Beaux-Arts detail on the elaborately carved stone used for this monumental depot. Is the building worth saving? Yes, definitely. But who pays, and how is the building to be used?

gines burned wood and coal. Despite spark arrestors and other devices, locomotives frequently set fire to depots, freight yards, and nearby buildings. Smoke fumes were poisonous and filled with soot and greasy particulates that covered depots as well as passengers. Diesel locomotives improved the atmosphere somewhat, but were still dirty and smelly. So a good railroad depot had to be a solid structure, one that could withstand the dirt, vibration, and the heavy wear and tear of large steamer trunks, crates of freight, and the occasional runaway locomotive.

A major station separated the passengers from the freight. In a large metropolitan area, freight handling was a completely separate function, located in a special freight depot away from passengers. Special accommodations needed to be made to handle various commodities. Refrigerator cars needed to be iced to keep perishables fresh; smelly cattle cars needed to be kept away from passengers. Roads and walkways had to be well built to carry trucks of baggage or freight between the waiting trains and the freight depots.

The toxic residues from tank cars, feedlots and other freight continue to plague railroad stations. Decades of coal or diesel fuel handling have saturated station yards with wastes that remain hazardous for years. It's an important engineering consideration, one that is frequently overlooked when evaluating a old depot site for retrofitting or reuse. That is, until state regulatory boards declare the station a candidate for a hazardous materials clean-up program.

Delight

This is the third measure of fitness and the one that is the most interesting to discuss. Your depot should pass the other two measures first, before you apply this one. However, a good depot should also meet this third test, and to make our task a little easier, we should define some of our aesthetic criteria.

Travel is an adventure, always a little exciting. That's why many of us like to travel for recreation. But we also like to feel safe and comfortable when we travel. We like to feel secure in our surroundings, and we like to feel welcomed, even when we don't know a soul in the town we are visiting. When we arrive at the gateway of our destination, we would like to know a little about the town, as soon as possible. We like to know the name of our host, for instance, even if our host is a place, not a person. We like a friendly smile, even if it is from a building and not a human.

A pretty depot says a lot about the values of the community and the quality of the hospitality that the town offers. It is important to try to meet a visitor's expectations; it makes travelers comfortable. Imagine arriving in New York or Chicago and stepping into a tiny boxcar of a waiting room. Or

Previous page: Waiting on the platform at Warrensburg, Missouri, can be entertaining. The elaborate detailing under the eaves provides visual amusement at this nicely restored depot. It also serves as the office for the Chamber of Commerce. Will detail like this ever be seen again on a new building? Highly unlikely. That's part of what makes such buildings worth preserving and restoring, the architecture, design, and finish work that will never be seen again in modern buildings.

The depot at Jackson, Michigan, shows what can be accomplished when Amtrak and the local community work together. This handsome brick building received a special present for its 100th birthday back in 1976. It was funded by matching grants from the State of Michigan and Amtrak. It reopened four years later and serves passengers on Amtrak's three Chicago-Detroit trains. *Robert Genat*

Every detail of the Jackson, Michigan, depot was carefully restored, including this cast iron columns supporting the roof over the original porte cochere. The exterior brick of the Jackson, Michigan, depot was cleaned and restored thanks to grants from Amtrak and the State of Michigan. Without such funding, however, fine work such as this might be left to rot or replaced by modern, unattractive structure and materials. *Robert Genat*

Next page: Even modern amenities like a plastic garbage container, a computer terminal, and a Coke machine can't rob an old depot like this one at Jackson, Michigan, of its understated elegance. It's unlikely that we would get to see such tall windows and such detailed wooden trim in any modern building. *Robert Genat*

dumping passengers and their baggage on a cold and icy platform alongside an open track in Colorado. Fortunately most depots that serve rail passengers make a special effort to make travelers feel comfortable. Some towns used the spaces on the sides of the depot as a garden park. Visitors would picnic while waiting for passengers arriving on the train.

It's a lot to ask of an inanimate structure, but a successful depot can say a lot about its surrounding community. At a glance it tells you about the local wealth, values, and age of the town. Is this a place that is secure in its identity, or is it a pretentious place that has built a depot that is too large to maintain? Is the building lovingly maintained, or does it have garish facelifts that have destroyed its charm?

You will recall that during the 1880s, railroad competition was at a peak. Some small towns had three or four depots, all built by competing railroads to acquire a major share of the market. Depots were used for advertising, and each depot building tried to demonstrate that the respective railroad was providing the safest, most modern, reliable, and comfortable travel experience available. Railroad architects put a great deal of consideration and expertise into designing a depot that would appeal to the customer. So, beyond the fads, the styles, the frosting...

Coke
EXIT

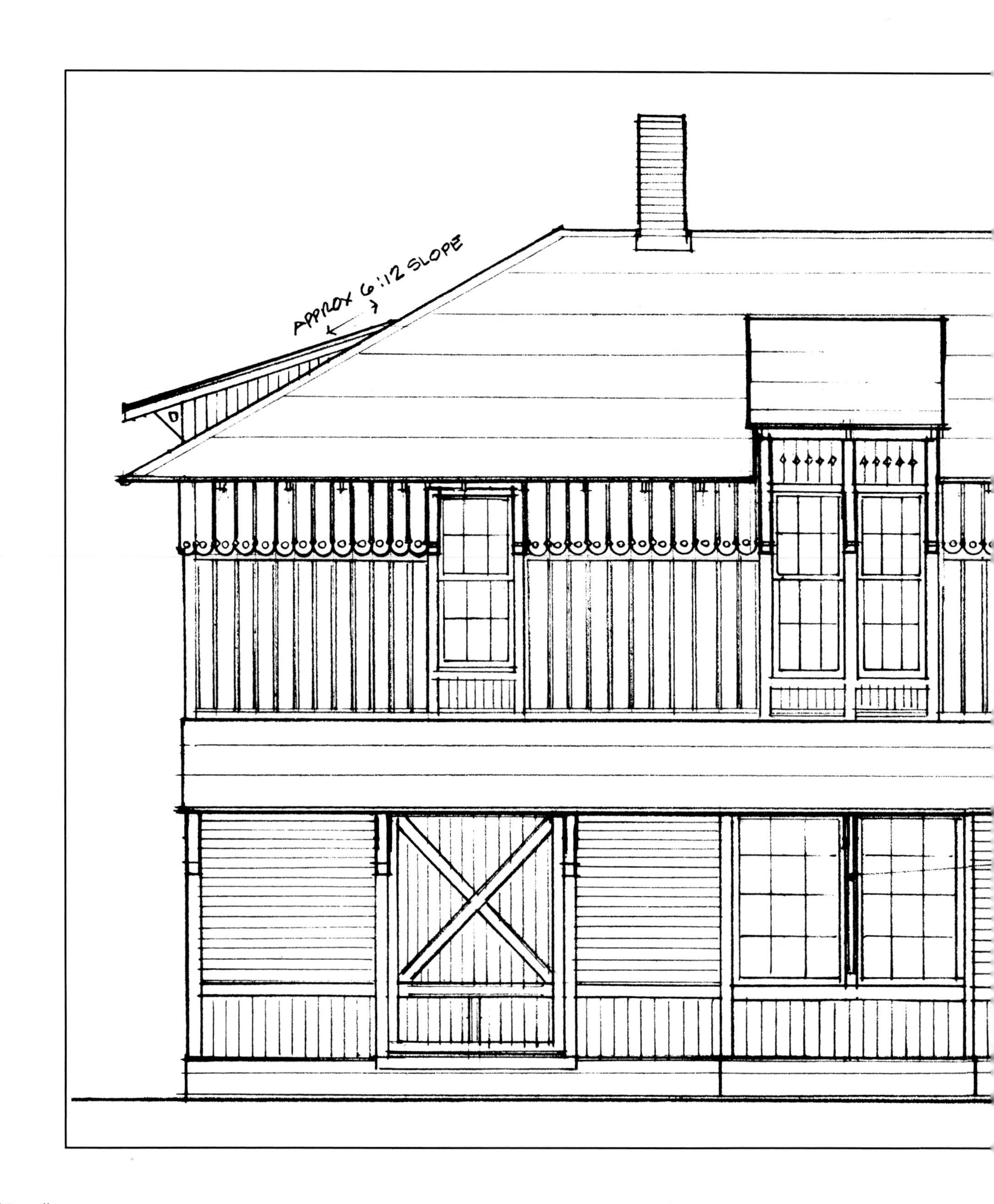
APPROX 6:12 SLOPE

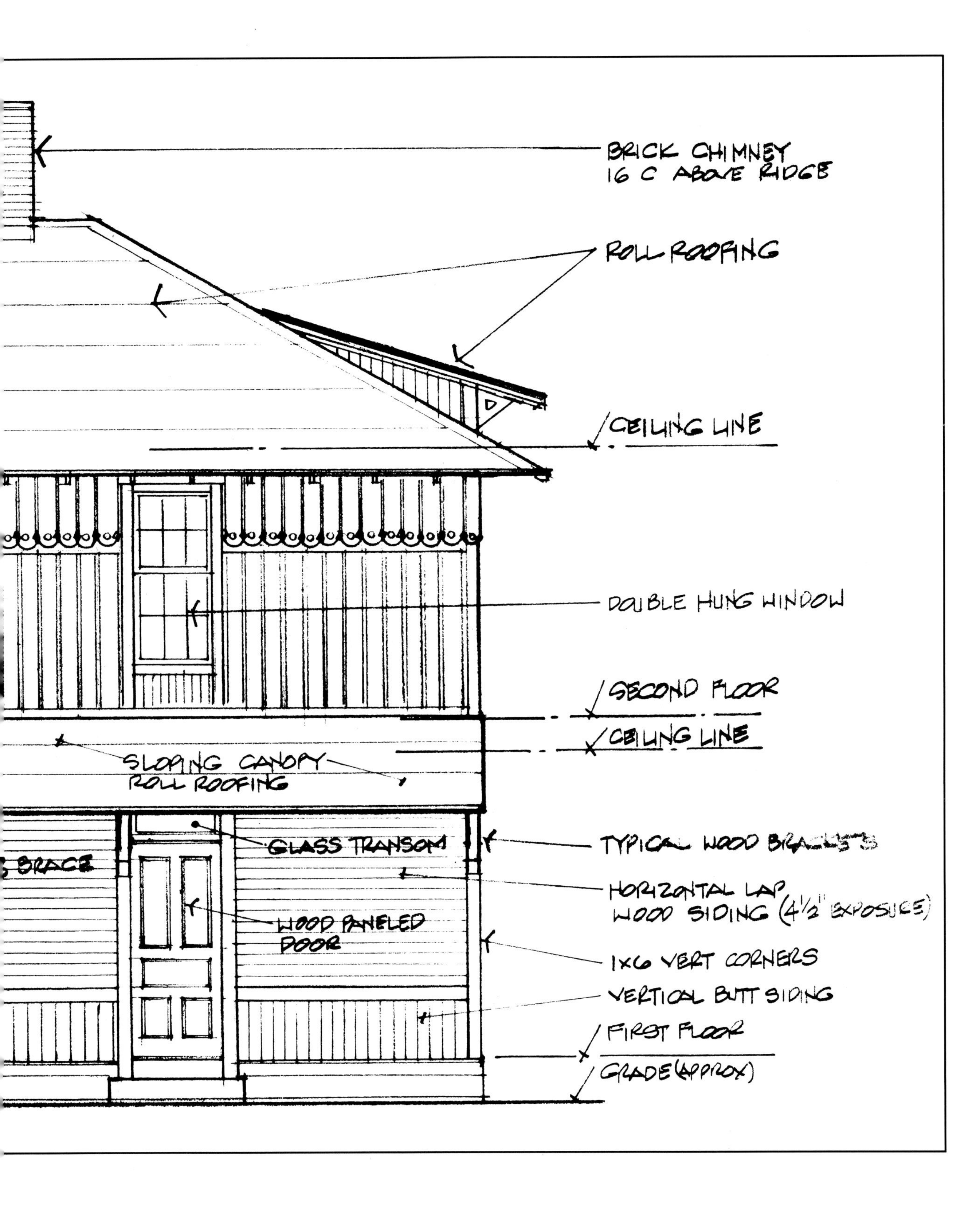

Here is the South Elevation of the C&A depot in Independence, Missouri. The depot is about 24 feet wide and 44 feet long, with a total interior floor space of about 2,200 square feet. It is a "balloon-frame" structure, with heavy timber rim joists and header joists, all supported by 24-inch square stone piers. The board pattern on the sides of the depot are called "stickwork." The ornamental treatment of the pierced boards form a frieze in what is known as Eastlake style. *George Lund & Associates, Architects*

how does this building make you feel? Do you feel safe, comforted, and welcomed? Do you feel that you have "arrived?"

Firmness, commodity, delight... those are the classic measures on the yardstick. But rail fans usually add two more categories; rarity and engineering. There are some old railroad buildings that have a very special appeal based on crazy criteria. So here are some additional considerations that might provide some insight into what justifies all the fuss.

Some kinds of depots, especially the smaller, more common ones like the boxcar depots, have virtually disappeared. Like the now extinct passenger pigeon, we presumed that since there were a lot of them around, a lot of them would stay around. So the experts really wave their arms when one of these fragile survivors are endangered. Rail fans also treasure any artifact from some of the smaller railroads with an interesting or unique history. The Yazoo and Mississippi Railroad comes to mind, so does the

Is it worth preserving? This "Amshack" in Pendleton, Oregon, doesn't seem to have great value, but down the road, especially if it's one of the few such structures still standing, it might be worth saving. As it is, such facilities are little more than glorified bus stops. Over time, though, they might be worth preserving—possibly to remind us of what *not* to aspire to.

Is it worth restoring? Does it meet the criteria for restoration or preservation attention and funding? If the building is of historical value, or if it's architecturally significant, then the answer is yes. But as is the case with this faded freight depot in Mojave, California, it sometimes takes a look beyond the aging surface to see a building's true value. It might take a look into the county historical society's records, or a consultation—perhaps gratis—by an architectural historian to help measure a depot's value.

Cornwall and Lebanon Railroad. Surviving depots from these lines are prized for their scarcity; sometimes they are the only remaining artifacts.

Depots that are the only remaining work of a prominent or interesting architect are treasured. Since many architects designed depot buildings hundreds of miles from their offices, local historians sometimes miss the importance. Marysville, Kansas, has a beautiful depot designed by Los Angeles architect Gilbert Stanley Underwood. And the spectacular Cheyenne, Wyoming, depot was designed by the Boston firm of Van Brunt and Howe. So sometimes the best work of an important American designer is far removed from the area where most of his commissions appear.

The last category is for engineering. And rail fans admire and appreciate engineering, and that includes trestles, tunnels, bridges, and some marvelous switchbacks. The Eads Bridge depot is a technical marvel. So are many of the railsheds and interlock towers. Rail fans admire engineers who have successfully merged terrain and trackage, fitting railroad facilities into the landscape, sometimes with great ingenuity. Any station that represents extraordinary efforts or a technological milestone in architectural engineering or design is given special attention. For instance, in St. Louis it's hard to know which is more impressive, the St. Louis Union Station or the 600-foot train shed. New York's Grand Central Station is incredible, but so is the magnitude of the engineering design beneath the streets.

And one last quirk... everyone seems to have a special place in their heart for the depot from their home town or a depot that bears their name. My mother has a postcard of her namesake depot at Libby, Montana, even though she has never visited the town. We all have our favorites.

A "witches' cap" is what this roof detail was called when it was a popular design element in chateau, Queen Anne, and other styles when they were in vogue.

Santa Fe
SHAWN

An All-American Style

The Santa Fe

The American West... the other railroads all went West but the Atchison, Topeka & Santa Fe was the only railroad to promote the West as a business product. The Santa Fe didn't just sell you a railroad ticket, it gave you adventure, romance, and the opportunity for an unforgettable experience. It transported you to another time as well as another place. The route, the food, the hotels, and the depots were all part of the package; entertaining, educational, and comfortable.

The Atchison, Topeka & Santa Fe was spawned in the usual way for the usual reasons: a regional system connecting communities with already established commercial ties. In this case those communities were at either end of the Santa Fe Trail; one end at Independence, Missouri, and the other end at Santa Fe, New Mexico. A brisk and profitable trade developed between the two communities in the early 1800s after Captain William Becknell organized a highly successful trade expedition. Wagon loads of manufactured goods were freighted to Santa Fe aboard big wagons hauled by oxen and loads of furs and precious metals returned from sources in Mexico.

A railroad was proposed in 1860, begun in 1868, and by 1872, the tracks had been laid across Colorado. A struggle for control of the railroad business developed between several competitors during the 1870s with the ultimate result that the AT&SF became a dominant force. By the 1880s their trackage extended from Chicago to the Pacific Ocean. It was a cut-throat period for the

You can almost hear children on the trains of yesterday talking excitedly about approaching "the castle" with its stone tower at Shawnee, Oklahoma. The marvelous stone structure was actually a Santa Fe depot, one which served travelers heading east from across the state, as well as riders from Kansas City and points east.

It's a Santa Fe depot. The trademark Santa Fe cross is featured on the tower at this interesting depot in Shawnee, Oklahoma.

railroad industry, with many companies going bankrupt or being swallowed up by other lines. Like the others, AT&SF struggled during the recession of the 1890s and fell into receivership. But by the turn of the century there was new management and a new attitude. The railroad had 11,000 miles of trackage and over 32,000 pieces of rolling stock. More important, they had some new talent in the head office.

A passenger traffic manager in Los Angeles named J. J. Byrne is credited with shortening the name to "Santa Fe" around the turn of the century. He came up with the idea about 1897, and there are several versions of the story of how the trademark Santa Fe cross first appeared, but it was quickly and widely accepted. This railroad was the Santa Fe... the Santa Fe Trail, the Conquistadors, the padres, the trail to gold, to adventure, to California, and to the missions.

The depot at Shawnee, Oklahoma is as quaint and charming as ever, thanks to a community that has preserved and protected the old Santa Fe stone structure. Trains no longer stop for passengers here, but people still stop by to visit; the depot today houses a museum.

Santa Fe, along with the other railroads, photographed every depot to document its property, a requirement of the Interstate Commerce Commission back around about 1915. This handsome bit of property, along with its chummy staff, once served Oceanside, California. In the days before the post office provided parcel service, this was the place you came to pick up your order from Sears Roebuck or Montgomery Wards. The depot agent here worked for Santa Fe, Wells Fargo, and Western Union, and sometimes the income from the freight business and telegraphs amounted to more than the railroad salary. *Atchison, Topeka, and Santa Fe- Kansas State Historical Society*

Fred Harvey and the Girls

The Santa Fe had an impressive railroad organization but so did the competition. However, the Santa Fe had one unique asset that no other railroad could offer... Fred Harvey and his girls. It was Fred Harvey and the Harvey restaurants and hotels that gave the Santa Fe its identity as the railroad of the West.

In the days before dining cars, after the Civil War and before 1880, trains stopped for meals at huge eating houses adjacent to the depots. The experience was, according to all reports, vile! The halts were typically only fifteen minutes long, the service was either brusque or non-existent, and the food was—everybody agreed—ghastly.

Travelers put up with a lot back then, including frequent accidents, Indian attacks, and slow speeds. They endured cars that were freezing in the winter, furnace-like in the summer and rattletraps all the time—but the quality of the food and the sleazy practices of the restaurant proprietors were a national scandal. Fred Harvey and the Santa Fe transformed that problem, together.

The change began quietly, at a little depot meal house at Topeka, Kansas, in 1876. The AT&SF provided the funding and Harvey provided the management for what was to be a radical experiment. The old meal stop was completely shut down for two days, scrubbed floor to ceiling, then restocked with high grade china and foodstuffs. Within a couple of weeks the place was a sensation, with capacity business from Topeka locals and delighted railroad passengers.

With the Topeka operation running smoothly, Harvey and the Santa Fe decided the next year to expand to the little town of Florence, just down the line. Harvey stocked it with the best, most expensive Irish linen, china, silver flatware, and the best chef

Interior, Fred Harvey lunchroom in the San Diego Union Station. Lunch here, on the day this photograph was made in 1915, cost about fifty cents (a bargain even then), was reliably delicious and generous, and would be served by a charming, handsome, and unmarried young lady specially trained for the job. The "Harvey girls" were credited with helping civilize the West. *Library of Congress*

he could find. Local farmers were recruited to supply fresh produce, eggs, milk and butter—at good prices. This food and the service became the Santa Fe's best advertising, and railroad ridership suddenly improved on AT&SF routes with Harvey House restaurants. Part of the attraction was the food, but another important feature was the service.

At first Harvey's meals were served by the same scruffy waiters that staffed restaurants all the time. Harvey soon replaced them, however, with a corps of specially trained young women who were trained and supervised especially for the job. The "Harvey Girls," as they were soon called, became another sensation all by themselves. Combined with the great food, it was an unbeatable combination.

Meals at first cost just fifty cents, a bargain even then, and prices went up to a dollar by 1900. The restaurants lost money as independent operations, but the increased ridership of the railroad more than made up for it. The restaurants pulled large numbers of passengers for the Santa Fe away from the competition. The Harvey Houses revolutionized more American business than just food service. They were the first chain restaurants, a model for many franchise operations to come. And they were the first example of a nationwide service standard; you could

expect the same level of courtesy and attention from any Harvey establishment you patronized.

Marketing the West

During the formative years, the AT&SF depot architecture was just as simple and dull as all the other railroads rolling track across the open prairie. The depots were stark and simple enclosures, built in a few days. They were as functional as a barn and built along the same lines; no need to put up anything fancy. In most cases the depot was the only building for miles around. The first depots were meant to be temporary. But westward travelers were soon to change all that. Hundreds of immigrant farmers and adventurers rode the Santa Fe in search of opportunity. The temporary depots needed to be replaced.

Newspapers and railroads had both paid travel journalists to create images of romance, adventure, and relaxation along the Santa Fe Trail as early as 1870. And soon the writers were joined by civic boosters in California, also extolling the climate and the scenery on the Pacific coast. But it was two writers who caught the public fancy that really spurred Western travel. The appearance of a popular novel by Helen Hunt Jackson titled "Ramona" set off a wave of interest in the Spanish missions, in mission life, the native Americans, and the West. And a popular journalist named Charles Fletcher Lummis marched from Cincinnati to the West Coast along the Santa Fe Trail, keeping armchair adventurers posted with his diary. Travelers became intrigued with the West.

Perhaps the Santa Fe discovered that it had tapped a nerve when it first printed a reproduction of Thomas Moran's landscape of "The Grand Canyon." Like the other railroads, the Santa Fe suffered in the economic depressions of the early 1890s and looked to advertising to increase consumer interest. In 1892, Santa Fe acquired exclusive reproduction rights to Moran's glorious landscape and soon the picture was hanging in depots all across the West. The railroad placed copies in hotels, schools, and any other establishment that could provide railroad business. The image of the Grand Canyon became associated with the Santa Fe style.

The Santa Fe seems to have always been a railroad with a lot of flair. In the 1880s one of the first Harvey Houses at Holbrook, Arizona, is reported to have been built of five boxcars. They were decorated with Indian motifs, but the tables were set with the same high quality linen and silver that diners had come to expect in a Harvey establishment. Santa Fe managers have always seemed to have a creative flair and an appreciation for

This grand establishment is one of the many and renowned Fred Harvey lunch rooms built alongside the Santa Fe tracks. This was a remarkable, important development, a partnership that transformed American food service very much for the better. Fred Harvey and the Santa Fe used high quality food, low prices, and charming architecture to lure passengers from other railroads. In fact, they pioneered the tourist industry by getting people to travel for the pleasure of it—and there wasn't much else to attract folks to Barstow, California, where this picture was made. *Atchison, Topeka, and Santa Fe collection—Kansas State Historical Society*

aesthetics. This quickly developed into the design philosophy for the development of their depots and their new depot hotels.

When the new president, Edward Ripley, took over the newly reorganized Santa Fe in 1896, he recognized the business potential in what was becoming known as the Santa Fe style, and elevated William H. Simpson to advertising manager. Simpson had worked for the Santa Fe for fifteen years and had worked hard to promote the scenic beauty of the attractions along the Santa Fe line. As a traffic manager, he had arranged rail travel for artists, trading trips in exchange for paintings that the railroad could use in its promotional material. Travel on the Santa Fe helped develop the art colonies at Taos and Santa Fe. It was corporate support of the artistic environment that brought out the best in appreciative designers. And one of the Santa Fe designers, Mary Colter, refined the Santa Fe style into an American style still defines our image of the American West.

Fred Harvey, Mary Colter, and the Santa Fe Style

Santa Fe and Fred Harvey enjoyed a curious business partnership. It was a handshake arrangement, with Fred Harvey running the restaurants and souvenir concessions, with the railroad building the depots and hotels. Consistent with this curious arrangement, Mary Colter was actually employed by the Fred Harvey Company and worked with their architect, but the actual engineering and construction was under the supervision and responsibility of the Santa Fe company construction engineers.

Mary Colter first went to work for the Santa Fe just after the turn of the century, when railroad travel was again increasing. Mission revival architecture, in depots in particular, had become very prevalent, due to the popularization of the novel "Ramona." By the late 1880s both the Southern Pacific Railroad and the Santa Fe marketed "Ramona Tours," an opportunity to tour the colorful missions in California and the Southwest. Many depots throughout the West were built in this style by all the railroads, and it was not unusual to see depots as far east as Illinois showing some of the Mission revival features.

The Santa Fe used depot architecture and native American art to enhance and support the travel experience. An excursion on the Santa Fe transported the traveler to another dimension as well as another place, via the magic of their talented architects and designers. The Harvey Company provided impeccable service and marvelous food in the depot hotels. The traveler could enjoy a complete and comfortable "Western experience," with picturesque natives offering crafts for sale, and hotels and dining rooms designed in the rancho style of the American Southwest. But these hotels had indoor plumbing, electricity, and cuisine that could only be matched in major cities. It was an enormous success, a concept that set the Santa Fe apart from all the other railroads. Today we call it Santa Fe style.

Mary Colter and architect Charles Whittlesey were assigned to build a new hotel in Albuquerque, to be named the Alvarado, after an early Spanish explorer Hernando de Alvarado. A Spanish style architecture seemed to offer an appropriate motif. So the hotel was designed with typical design features of a Spanish hacienda such as a red-tiled roof and a long, mission style arcade between the depot and the new hotel.

The Alvarado featured the latest hotel amenities for 1902, including electric lighting, steam heating, and a barber shop. But it also featured something new, something that was to set a standard and redefine the Santa Fe style. Located adjacent to the arcade between the depot and the hotel, the new attraction was an Indian Building. Mary Colter designed the interior to display native American art to its best advantage. It was part museum and part gift shop, and Fred Harvey and the Santa Fe had begun to foster and promote an appreciation of native American culture and crafts. The museum contained a replica of a Hopi religious altar, displayed behind locked gates. Native Americans could be visited in the Indian Building, at work weaving or making jewelry. And tourists could then purchase art or a souvenir at the Indian Building gift shop.

The Santa Fe had a growing collection of paintings of the Southwest but the Fred Harvey Company had also collected native American artifacts. The Harvey collection of Indian blankets was displayed at the 1904 St. Louis Exposition. While Santa Fe manager William Simpson had been commissioning Southwestern landscapes and illustrations of native American life for more than a decade, the Harvey Company had been collecting blankets, pottery, jewelry, baskets, and other artifacts for nearly as long. The opportunity to build a second Indian Building soon arrived.

Mary Colter's second railroad hotel, museum, and gift shop was called Hopi House, located at the rim of the Grand Canyon. Once again Charles Whittlesey provided the architectural framework and Mary Colter designed the atmosphere.

It was built at the site of the El Tovar, one of the first resort hotels in the southwest. Not accessible by roads, the area opened to tourists when the Santa Fe acquired a little bankrupt spur line. The fabulous scenery provided a unique opportunity to

One of the last passenger depots built in the U.S. was this Santa Fe depot in Lawrence, Kansas. It was built in the 1950s, when lots of University of Kansas college students made the trek from home to school on the train. Its architecture is moderne style, and it's easily mistake for a converted bank or small-town clinic. It's a far cry from the grand Union Stations, and there's certainly no room for the Harvey girls to work their magic.

build a hotel, and the Santa Fe had featured Thomas Moran's painting of the Grand Canyon for a decade. So it was a natural opportunity for Santa Fe and the Harvey Company.

The El Tovar was opened in 1905, a 100-room hunting lodge, decorated with hunting trophies and Indian pottery. It was a curious style of architecture but an extremely suitable style of building for its locale, a grand but rustic Western lodge. Directly across from the lodge was Hopi House, a combination museum, gift shop, and workshop for native American art. Built in the style of a Hopi village, this multilevel stone building originally had dwellings on the upper levels. Hopis who worked in the building lived on the upper floors.

Mary Colter went on to refine what we now call Santa Fe style, using design elements from native American crafts and blending them with local history in her depot hotels. She created design themes by creating a fictional history for some of her projects. The station hotel in Winslow, Arizona that was known as La Posada, was entirely an invention of her imagination. She visualized the depot and hotel as the rancho of one of the Spanish dons, and then designed an interior to match the taste of this wealthy but imaginary individual. She mixed Spanish antiques and colorful tiles, mirrors with pierced tin frames from Mexico and hand-hewn benches. The overall effect was a rancho fantasy. The traveler became a privileged guest in a fairy tale casa.

It was a unique blend of commercialism and Southwestern romanticism that worked to the advantage of the railroad, the traveler, and the local economy. The Santa Fe railroad and the Harvey House hotel continued to develop this extraordinary partnership, setting new standards in depot design and comfort. The Santa Fe also defined the Southwest to the remainder of Americans, preserving and promoting native cultures in a way that no other railroad and no other business has ever attempted.

For many of us, the words Santa Fe Super Chief recall the adventure of travel on the first all-diesel, all-Pullman passenger train across the southwest. In our mind's eye we can see the familiar Super Chief profile in a war bonnet, a symbol of Santa Fe pride and spirit. Maybe a few of us were fortunate enough to enjoy the complete experience, travel on a railroad that celebrated native American art right down to the Mimbreno designs on the coffee cups in the dining cars. Leaving the train for a short excursions we could visit magnificent scenery and appreciate local crafts, again courtesy of the Santa Fe railroad. And the travel experience is an adventure that calls us back. We want to come again and experience the magic, as soon as we have the chance. It's the super, super Santa Fe Super Chief.

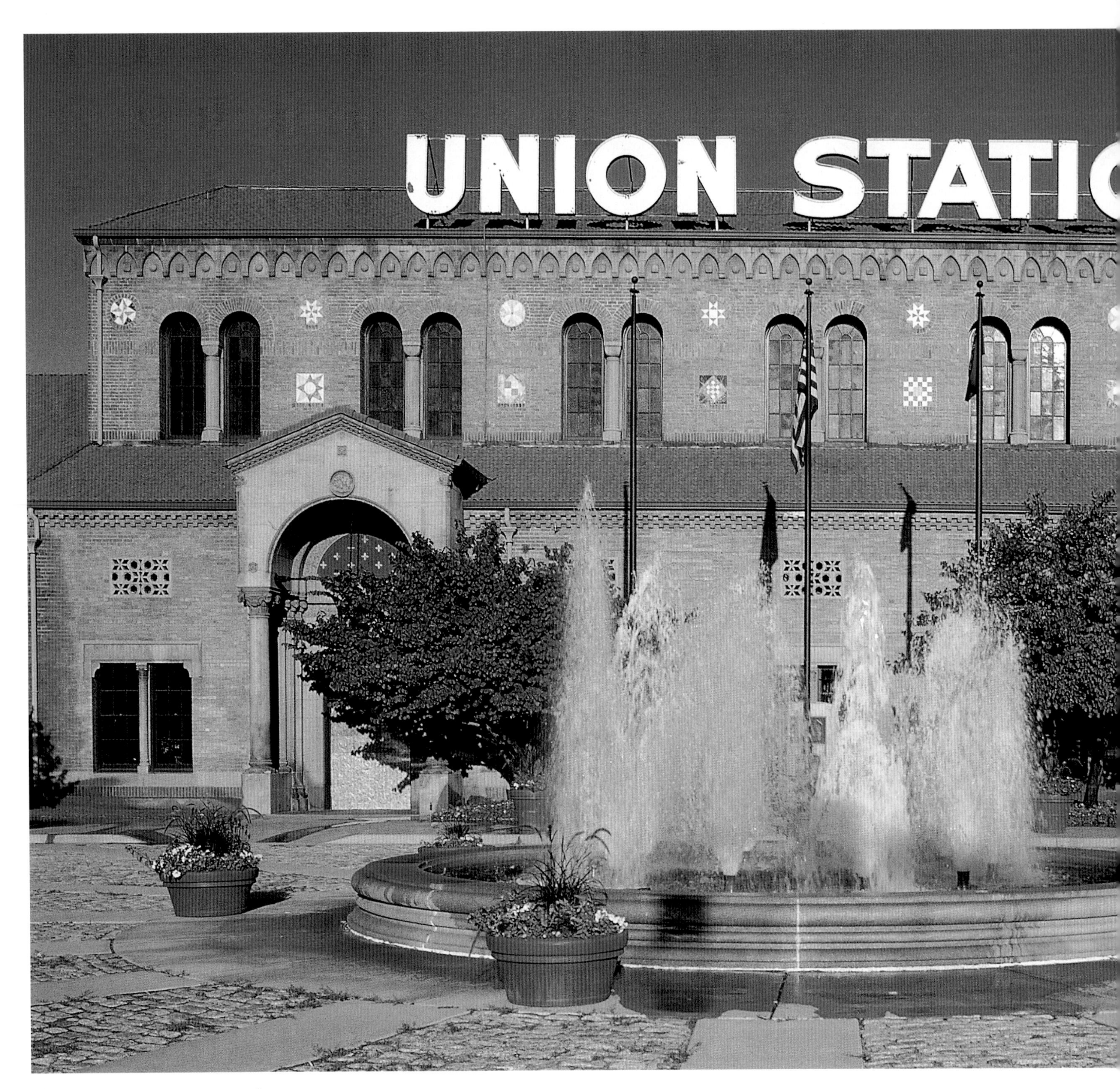
UNION STATIO

The Union Terminals

The Grand Arrival

Going to the City... you really arrived when you stepped off the train. In the age of industry the railroad station somehow became a symbol of civic identity. Small towns all had depots but when you went to the Big City... you usually got off the train at a terminal, the end of the railroad line.

A large, ornate railroad terminal depot was a symbol of urban wealth, technical development, and cultural sophistication. A railroad terminal could say something about a town that a City Hall or a Cathedral could not.

It started as rivalry among the railroads. Building a bigger, better terminal meant that you could usually attract more customers. All of the railroads were competing for business, passengers and freight. Little thought was given to the impact that three or four or a dozen terminals would have on one city.

In the beginning it was England once again that built the first terminals. Europeans were first to observe what happened when rail lines occupied the center of town. Railroads brought tremendous wealth into town, and loads of raw materials and manufactured goods could be shipped directly from the factories to the ports. But it made a jumble of the old cities with narrow streets, loaded the air with soot and cinders, and burned down a few buildings.

It quickly became evident that railroads would need more space, with separate terminals to serve passengers and freight. Trains, stagecoaches, wagons, and pedestrians were all

Ogden, Utah's Union Station is a glittering example of a nicely restored depot that has been recycled to do what such a building does best—serve railroad passengers.

competing for the same space. A stalled wagon could delay a train. Passengers were understandably reluctant to travel in dirty, dangerous facilities.

The Passenger Terminal Depots

Railroad terminal construction was slowed by the Civil War, but Americans quickly made up for lost time. Historian Carroll Meeks points out that there were no terminals to rival European ones until William H. Vanderbilt built his first Grand Central Terminal in 1872. So we should probably credit Vanderbilt for first elevating the American railroad terminal to status as a civic monument. The New York terminal was the symbol for the Vanderbilt railroads, and the New York Central railroad terminal building became a symbol for the urban sophistication in the city of New York.

Vanderbilt's concept for a terminal design was a logical one. In 1871 he combined passenger access to all of his railroad lines that terminated in New York City. He built Grand Central Terminal to house the New York Central & Hudson River Railroad, the New York & Harlem Railroad, and the New York & New Haven Railroad. It was a signature building, one that promoted all Vanderbilt lines and other railroads in other major American cities took notice. The Age of the Grand Terminal had begun.

The Age of the Grand Terminal set off a wave of Union Terminal construction in most large American cities. These were second generation depots, built to replace one or sometimes several smaller passenger depots. Many were financed in a cooperative manner, rather than by an individual railroad. In addition, most Union Terminals were built with some degree of encouragement and cooperation of the local community. Although the stations covered an entire city block with the railshed taking up another city block or two, it usually meant that the dirt and noise of a railroad could be contained within a smaller area of the city.

The Grand Terminals were a terminal, the end of the line. The trackage ended at the railhead. Characteristics of the typical Union Terminal include size, layout, and methods of financing. They served more than one rail line, although in many cases they were a connecting point between a trunk line and a suburban railroad, also owned by the same railroad. They were a transfer point for passengers, and they tried to offer the passenger some comfort and amenities while waiting for the train. Construction of the passenger terminal depots was an important high water mark for the railroads. The traveling public had never before (and never since) had such personal consideration and construction money lavished on them.

Plans and sketches of a few of the Union Terminals appear in a railroad engineering textbook by Walter G. Berg published in 1893. About forty-six terminals appear in the text, all built in the two decades between 1872 and 1892. Only a handful of Grand Terminals survive from this first wave of terminal construction; the St. Louis Union Station (1894) and the Indianapolis Union Station (1888) are two notable examples. Most of the first Grand Passenger Terminal Depots, as they were called, were torn down to accommodate even grander depots.

Grand Central and The Pennsylvania Station

In retrospect, we now fully realize that the appearance of the two magnificent New York terminals represent an especially glorious moment in the Golden Age of railroad building. It's a tale of two old American cities and their railroad empires. For a brief moment two historic rivals, the Vanderbilt roads and the Pennsylvania interests, once again struggled to dominate the eastern railroad network.

The Pennsylvania Station represented the City of Philadelphia and the Pennsylvania Railroad. Philadelphia, once called the Venice of the West, had been America's first center of commerce, art, and science. The Pennsylvania Railroad, founded in 1846, was the largest railroad in the world, still the national leader, setting the standards by which all other railroads were judged.

Opened in 1910, the late great Pennsylvania Station was the terminal that opened New York's eyes to new vistas. Railroad president Alexander Cassatt had a deep appreciation for the arts and had spent much time in Europe. His favorite sister, Impressionist painter Mary Cassatt, lived in France. He had visited Italy on one of his many trips abroad, and had been impressed by the Baths of Caracalla and the temple of Diocletion, public buildings that were light and airy. When presented with the opportunity to build a new terminal building, he chose European-trained architect Charles McKim. who had also been impressed by Roman architecture, especially the Baths.

This unique terminal would demonstrate that art and engineering were complementary disciplines. Design and construction took nearly a decade. Cassatt had decided to dig four single-track tunnels under the East River and two single-track tunnels under the Hudson River to allow trains to approach the station underground. The terminal building would appear in the cityscape as a calm and classic monument; the noisy, dirty bustle of the locomotives and the tracks would be hidden underground.

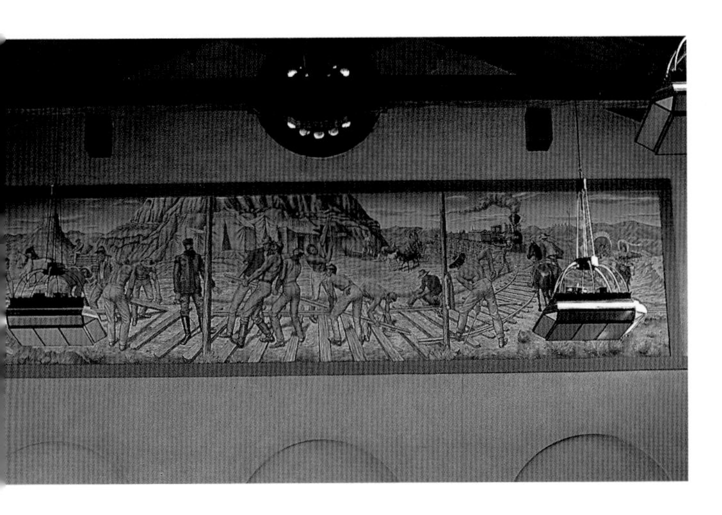

Previous page: Cheyenne, Wyoming, is and always has been a railroad town, and the Union Pacific is still the focus of the community. The UP built their hometown depot big and bold, and it has served many generations of travelers. When this photograph was made the terminal was undergoing a through cleanup and renovation.

Left: The historic mural became a feature of many Union Terminals. This one appears in the Ogden, Utah, depot, which was built in 1909. Such murals were as close to fine art as most rural people ever came during the early years of the century. Like the frescoes in other kinds of cathedrals, these paintings were designed to both charm and inform the viewer of a particular world view.

Right: The entrance to the depot in Ogden, Utah, has little golden stars that twinkle in the sky blue mosaic. This handsome Union station has been beautifully restored to very nearly original condition, inside and out. The Parkinsons carefully designed every detail in the depot. All of the light fixtures, all of the furniture and many of the interior features are custom designed, works of art from an age when America could afford such luxury.

The St. Louis Union Station project succeeded because private and public people, money, and interests cooperated to develop a single vision. It took years, $180 million, and the efforts of hundreds of people, but it seems to have paid off.

Grand Central Station represented New York City, the Vanderbilt empire, and the second largest trunk line in America, the New York Central. New York had overtaken and replaced Philadelphia as the banking and commercial center of America. Now it was becoming the passenger transportation center as well, bringing travelers into the very heart of the island of Manhattan without a time-consuming ferry ride.

The first Vanderbilt Terminal was an overwhelming success, but it was now more than thirty years old. Enormous advancements in technol-

ogy were taking place in the 1890s and it was now possible to use electricity to power rail travel.

The first building had become technologically obsolete; the replacement structure was part of a gigantic transportation network powered solely by electricity. It was now possible to enter New York

City on an electric railroad and then transfer to an electric subway to see the sights.

Grand Central Station advertised itself as The Terminal City. It was once estimated that 3,000 people worked at the terminal every day, in the shops, restaurants, and offices. Their advertising boasted that they could accommodate 30,000 people a day in this "city within a city" covering 30 square blocks in New York City. Over a thousand railroad cars could be accommodated at one time. A building this size, with this many people coming and going, attracted a few bums, thieves, and hangers-on. Newspaper reporters were known to regularly drop by the coffee shop. So did the beat officers. It was bigger than most small towns in America.

The two terminal buildings also represent an important new level in railroad engineering. Both buildings were designed by architects whose work is still recognized as masterpieces of American design. The two buildings were under construction about the same time; one was opened in 1910, the other in 1913. And both opened new frontiers of railroad engineering. Grand Central had an all-electrical network with two levels of underground trackage; 41 tracks on the upper level, 26 on the lower level. The Pennsylvania railroad had opted to tunnel under two rivers to bring its lines directly into Manhattan, eliminating the need for ferry boats. There has been

Perhaps the most ambitious and successful railroad depot restoration is St. Louis' magnificent 1894 rockpile, still a showplace, still serving rail passengers, and providing a wide variety of services to thousands of people daily.

N.Y. CENTRAL & HUDSON R.R.R.
NEW-YORK & HARLEM R.R.
NEW-
BROADWAY
ASTOR PLACE

no other achievement of this magnitude in American rail history.

Grand Central lives on, still serving New Yorkers. The adjacent Post Office building is about to become a major Amtrak station project. Soon cross-country rail passengers will once again be able to arrive in the middle of Manhattan. The great Pennsylvania Station lives on too, although the structure was demolished in 1963 to make way for the Madison Square Garden arena. The Pennsylvania station lives on in photographs and memories, but, most important, it lives on in the determination of dozens of groups who are now committed to the preservation of other depots and terminals.

The 1963 demolition of the Pennsylvania Station was a turning point for historic preservation. Disgusted by speculative development and appalled by weak-kneed politicians, thousands of Americans became personally involved in preserving old buildings. The demolition became a catalyst that changed the way government agencies operate. Cities, states, and federal projects now require a comprehensive Environmental Impact Report that looks at all aspects of removing a historic building. You could say that the Pennsylvania Terminal saved the life of the Grand Central. Ten years later, Grand Central too was endangered. But citizens rallied and the building was saved, remembering their experience with the Pennsylvania Terminal.

Until this building was constructed, the City of New York was served by the New York and New Haven, the New York Central, and the New York & Harlem, each with independent depots, each serving just one line. Commodore Cornelius Vanderbilt is credited with building a single unified terminal for them all, and here it is, the first Grand Central Station. The terminal was built between 1869 and 1871 and transformed the concept of the American urban depot forever. *Library of Congress*

Here's an artist's rendition of the St. Louis, Missouri, station when it opened in 1894. The magnificence of the structure is enhanced in the drawing because that there are no other buildings squeezing up against the depot or its adjacent streets. It's as if it's set back on it own huge estate while in reality it sits in the midst of an urban area. *Library of Congress*

The grand rotunda of Cincinnati's depot building doesn't handle the hordes of travelers who used to jam the place during World War II, but at least it is preserved in relatively pristine condition as it begins a second career as a museum. Unlike most such renovations, this project was financed by a county tax levy that generated $42 million. *Cincinnati Historical Society*

Next page: One of the very last and one of the very most expensive union stations built in America, the Cincinnati, Ohio, terminal opened in 1933 and cost over $20 million depression-era dollars. It served rail travelers for many years, then was transformed to serve the community as a science museum in the 1980s. It remains an Amtrak stop. *Cincinnati Historical Society*

Terminal Wars... Beaux Arts and the City Beautiful

When Union passenger terminals, or Union Stations, as they came to be called, were built, depot buildings had been in the urban landscape about fifty years. The traveling public expected to find certain services such as a coffee shop or restaurant at the depot. Although the depot was not a public building like the city hall or courthouse, and was owned and operated by a railway, it was nevertheless, a building where anyone could go at anytime.

To be a first-class, top-notch Union Station, the depot was expected to provide a variety of services. In fact, comfortable accommodations and various services had come to be expected, part of the amenities that the traveling public had grown to expect and therefore require. To serve waiting passengers, the depot should have several waiting rooms. It should offer a men's waiting room, a women's waiting room, a waiting room for emigrants, and a waiting room for "colored." An additional ladies parlor and a smoking room were highly desirable.

Since most of the Union Terminals provided passenger service for more than one railroad, you could expect to find separate ticket stands for each line. You could also buy tickets for local and suburban lines at their respective counters. And sometimes, if you had the time, you could make arrangements to do some local sightseeing.

There were a few very basic services that you expected to find near the large waiting room: a barber shop, a shoe-shine stand, a newspaper stand that also sold candy and tobacco, and the public telephones. In addition, several restaurants were desirable. You expected to find some sort of coffee shop that was open around the clock. It served waiting cab drivers as well as late-arriving travelers. Railroad employees usually had their own lunchrooms at the terminal,

Durand, Michigan, about 1905. This handsome building served forty-two passenger, twenty-two mail, and seventy-eight freight trains a day when it was new, back in 1903—when it was built at a cost of $60,000. It burned to the ground just eighteen months later—and was rebuilt to the same plan in only five months. Six trains pose for the camera at the spot where the Grand Trunk met the Ann Arbor railroad. You'll see this depot in its current, restored condition in chapter 2. *Library of Congress*

hidden away from view. And an elegant, full-service restaurant was usually included for visitors who wanted more than just coffee shop fare. The restaurant frequently had a cocktail lounge; serious drinkers went across the street to a saloon or pub at a neighboring hotel.

Really large terminals in major metropolitan areas had many rooms that the general public never saw. Most terminals had office space for various senior railroad managers; the senior freight agent, the right-of-way manager, and the division maintenance supervisor all frequently had offices on the top floors. So did the superintendent of the railroad mail service, the superintendent of the sleeping car services, and the railroad detectives.

If you were a member of a special segment of the traveling public, there might be separate accommodations available just for you. Special and separate rooms were set aside for visiting dignitaries, royalty, the President of the United States, and movie stars. But convicts arriving by rail got separate treatment too... so did dead bodies. Some terminals had a hospital with a physician on duty; some had customs officers with detention rooms for arriving emigrants.

Many terminals had a library or reading room, others had a YMCA on the premises. There are several stories about the first appearance of a YMCA in a terminal. Once source credits the Vanderbilts with the establishment of the railroad YMCA. Cornelius Vanderbilt is said to have identified himself with YMCA activities and for years he personally headed the branch that existed on his railroads. Other railroad historians say that the railroad YMCA was first established in Cleveland, Ohio, about 1872. Most sources agree that safe, decent lodging for railroad workers was needed and the railroad Y became an important institution in most major terminals.

Across the state of Missouri from St. Louis stands the monumental Kansas City Union Station, empty for twenty years, an example of civic bickering and poor planning. Only the efforts of a small group of preservationists saved this Beaux-Arts depot from the wrecking ball, and that is an important first step. Legal clearance to restore the building for public use was delayed until 1994, and a reopening of the old station isn't likely before the year 2000.

Topeka, Kansas, turned out for the opening of this building, its pride and joy, on January 28th, 1928. Today it stands empty and partly gutted by fire, although a community group is working to protect and preserve the handsome Union Pacific depot.

Union terminals frequently featured a clock tower after the railroad introduced standard time in 1888. This tower on the St. Louis, Missouri, Union Station was visible for miles away.

The general traveling public never saw the spaces reserved for railroad uses either. Baggage, Railway Express and the U.S. Mail had their own facilities at the depot. There were janitor's closets, fire-service apparatus closets, and walk-in refrigerators for all the restaurants. There were storage areas for ice, coal, groceries, and clean linen that would be put aboard the Pullman coaches. There were private apartments for the night watchman and maintenance engineers, those invisible people who kept the heaters, plumbing, and electrical systems in operating order.

Like the shopping mall of today, the Union Station was a place where you could meet someone, even if you were not traveling. "Meet me under the clock," it was a common and accepted practice. And at midnight on New Year's, all the partygoers in town showed up to watch the clock at midnight. And you could get a cab home easily!

Washington, D.C.

As a courtesy to the American taxpayer we include the Union Station from our nation's capital, one Union Terminal that has had to be rescued twice. Designed by Beaux Arts architect Daniel Burnham, it was originally opened in 1906, one of the many Union Stations built in that era that were expressions of the City Beautiful movement.

Like the other urban temples of the time, it was a "city within a city," sparing no expense to include every amenity imaginable. Knowing that this Union Station must be adequately prepared to serve royalty and international heads of state, it provided suitable accommodations for every contingency. Facilities included several state reception rooms, a nursery, and a bowling alley! Like other Union Stations it had several restaurants, walk-in refrigerators, and a hospital. Unlike other terminals, it needed 5,000 people to operate.

Efforts were made to keep this station from accelerated deterioration, but early plans were inappropriate and underfunded. In the late 1960s the government spent $48 million dollars to turn the Union Station into a Visitor's Center for the Capital, but the project failed badly. Finally, in 1981, Congress passed the Union Station Redevelopment Act. It took five years and another $160 million to restore, and today it serves as the corporate headquarters for Amtrak.

Cincinnati

Like most other mid-American cities at the turn of the century, Cincinnati had more than one major depot. Cincinnati had three terminals, several smaller depots, and a number of stations with depots in the surrounding suburban communities. The "Queen City" was an active river town with a healthy riverboat commerce and had vigorous railroad development a decade before the Civil War.

Cincinnati railroads suffered through the same economic depression and consolidations in the 1890s that affected the rest of the nation. And some attempts were made to eliminate stations that were not needed. But twenty years later, it was still served by seven railroads: the Baltimore & Ohio, the Ohio State Limited, the Pennsylvania Railroad, the Chesapeake & Ohio, the L & N, the Southern and the N & W. In spite of consolidations over the years, these seven railroads now used five separate passenger terminals, an arrangement that was inconvenient and awkward.

Railroad passenger traffic had grown, but so had freight and commercial traffic. Clearly Cincinnati needed new terminals badly and the obvious solution was to separate the two functions. A new passenger terminal was discussed and planned in the 1900s, but World War I delayed efforts. Development began in earnest after 1920, and the Union Station opened in 1933.

It was the grandest Union Terminal in the country, called the last great Union Terminal in the United States. It cost $41 million, a new record, and was supposed to handle 216 trains a day. Construc-

Union stations were advertisements for the companies that built and used them, and they were built for the ages. Consequently, railroads tended to tuck their corporate logo in just about anywhere it would fit, in this case on each end of the Union Pacific's Topeka, Kansas, depot.

Grand Central Station in New York City accommodates a tidal wave of humanity every day, morning and evening. Pennsylvania Station's destruction in the early 1960s so shocked Americans that the planned demolition of Grand Central and hundreds of other stations was averted. *Piet Halberstadt*

First a word about AMTRAK...

Amtrak passenger service is a significant presence in many of our remaining depots across America. However, in an effort to provide passenger service at reasonable cost, Amtrak actually owns very few facilities. In most depots the Amtrak service is only a tenant, leasing office space and attempting to provide some personal services to passengers. But while Amtrak actually owns very little real estate, they are it is a major player in the future vitality of urban centers. In most major cities and many smaller communities, Amtrak represents the federal agency that is providing critical leadership in the development of urban mass transit.

Passenger traffic is only about 7 percent of all rail service, and passengers are more expensive to haul than a load of coal, so railroads spend money to serve industrial customers, not passengers. Railroads tried for years to abandon passengers, pointing out that automobiles cars, buses, and planes had already taken most of the passenger market. After years of negotiating, the federal government worked out a compromise, and Amtrak was born in 1971. Amtrak was not supposed to succeed; passenger traffic was supposed to quietly fade away.

In the beginning, it seemed doomed to fail simply because of the difficulties in coordinating a coast-to-coast rail route. Most passengers are totally unaware that railroads are regional, that they compete with one another, and that they are vastly differing corporations. To many Americans, especially those that grew up with cars and planes, you just point the car down the highway and go. The idea that you would need permission to drive the freeway of another state seems ridiculous.

So when Amtrak was first started, it had to ask permission from dozens of railroads to use rail lines. And the railroads were asked to make passenger trains a priority, letting Amtrak trains go ahead of freight traffic. In addition, Amtrak wanted the best routes into the best cities. Amtrak wanted trunk routes with destinations in the heart of urban centers. It took a while to develop a national American rail passenger network, and it took a little longer to succeed. But there is no longer a question that it will fade quietly away.

Amtrak watches every nickel and keeps expenses low. And depots cost a lot to maintain for just a few passengers. So in some communities, even ones like Warrensburg or Pleasant Hill or Lee's Summit, all Missouri towns with lovely restored depots, the Amtrak train does not even use the depot. Passengers are dropped at the original platform but the shelter is an "Amshack." Nevertheless, Amtrak maintains a very important railroad presence in a community .

tion had started in August of 1929, just before the historic stock market crash. A depressed economy decreased the demand for passenger travel and the Union Terminal was never fully utilized. Another change in national lifestyles was more damaging to the terminal's success. The automobile had already made a serious dent in railroad passenger travel. Rail passenger travel peaked around 1924 and had been declining for a decade by the time the Cincinnati Union Terminal was opened.

By 1973 the Union Terminal was scheduled for demolition. The last of the passenger service had ended in 1972, and the building stood vacant for eight years before being opened as a shopping mall. It became the home for the Cincinnati Museum in 1990.

Los Angeles

It's difficult to understand what the engineers were really thinking when the Los Angeles Union Pacific Terminal was planned. A "Gateway to the West"... how could you enter California without a proper gateway at the City of the Angels? It must have been all of the sunshine and Hollywood dazzle that blinded them to a few obvious realities.

In spite of a depression, growth of the airline industry, and rapidly expanding automobile usage, plans to build a Union Station went right along. It opened in 1939 and cost only $11million, peanuts compared to the $41million price tag on the Cincinnati terminal, but those were depression-era dollars. At its peak it only saw thirty-three trains a day, and like all of the other Union Terminals, it fell into disrepair and gradual disuse.

Unlike eastern cities, Los Angeles saw no real need to establish a Terminal Railway Association to merge railroad traffic through the city. So the Santa Fe, the Southern Pacific, and the Union Pacific all steamed through town, tying up traffic and causing major traffic problems. There had been complaints for years and litigation that began in 1915. The lawsuits pitted the railroads against the city and eventually involved the California Railroad Commission, the California Supreme Court, and finally the Interstate Commerce Commission and the United State Supreme Court. The City of Los Angeles finally won in 1931.

But the railroads were starting to see the results of the Depression and asked for a delay. Los Angeles offered a million dollars to begin construction. The railroads took the money and still delayed. Construction started in 1933 and was finally complete by 1939. Designed by Donald and John Parkinson in the Spanish Mission revival style that has come to characterize Southern California, it is a masterwork of architecture. It includes all of the typical features that we expect in a Union Station: the Harvey House, a clock tower, an elegant waiting room and all the shops. But not even the most elegant design could save this terminal. After languishing like so many other stations in other downtowns, its future now depends on life as a commuter rail terminal. And like many other major metropolitan terminals, it has been restored and refurbished to become what is sometimes called a multi-modal transportation center.

St. Louis

Ask any traveler "What's the most wonderful depot you have ever seen?" Most of them respond, "St. Louis." Since "geography is destiny," the City of St. Louis occupies a very special location in America. It sits at the junction of the Missouri and Mississippi rivers and it is the Gateway to the West. Riverboats would come up the river from New Orleans and unload passengers who wanted to go West. Conscious of their unique role as an American gateway, St. Louis sponsored an international design competition for its terminal. Other mid-American cities had built depots; Indianapolis had one in 1886, Cincinnati had so much rail traffic that it had three Union Terminals by 1890. Kansas City built its first Union Terminal in 1878. But St. Louis wanted something better than all of these. So the St. Louis Terminal Railway Association, a consortia of the trunk railroads in St. Louis sponsored a design contest.

Although there were entrants from all over America and Europe, Link & Cameron, a St. Louis design firm, took the prize with a design that celebrated the French heritage of St. Louis. Link and Cameron proposed a building that looked like a magnificent chateau along the Loire, a radically different style than the Richardsonian terminal buildings in eastern America. Finished in 1894, it accommodated 31 rail lines.

This extraordinary terminal makes an important statement about the frontier and the development of American cities. It is a demonstration that St. Louis, in the heart of America, had reached a size and cultural sophistication that could provide the highest degree of engineering expertise and craftsmanship. Local artisans provided the interior finish work. St. Louis provided not only first-rate architects, but also first-rate artisans for the stained glass window, which was manufactured by the St. Louis firm of Davis & Chambers. Another St. Louis firm, Healy & Millet,

Grand Central still functions pretty much as intended when it was designed many years ago and still accommodates large numbers of people. Buildings like this are "gateway" structures, introducing visitors to the city, and were intended to make a good impression. *Piet Halberstadt*

The clock atop the central information booth, Grand Central station. Even as today's modern, plastic illuminated signs dot the depot, there's no denying its grace with elements such as this clock, with all its ornate detail. *Piet Halberstadt*

provided the frescos in the Grand Hall. The building was a triumph and the pride of St. Louis for decades. Dozens of shops lined the arcade behind the Grand Hall. Travelers and residents alike strolled the arcade to browse, to meet friends, and to visit. It was like strolling the Champs Elysee, except you were sheltered away from the weather. It was probably one of America's first indoor malls and became a model for light, airy, entertaining indoor public space.

The terminal in the 1960s needed help. It was renovated with $140 million in grants and loans and reopened in 1985. When it was reopened, it was the most expensive rehabilitation project to date. Since that time other terminal restorations have exceeded that price.

Kansas City

"Everything's up to date in Kansas City" and the Union Terminal was no exception. Beaux Arts was the current popular style for terminals and Kansas City was in desperate need of a new building. There were several depots already; a big Union Terminal had been built in the 1880s down by the river. But prosperous Kansas City was growing fast, eight rail lines came into town, and periodic flooding from the Kaw and Missouri rivers slowed terminal operations. A new terminal in a new location would bring additional business expansion. Besides, St. Louis Union Station was aging prematurely, a victim of the rapid development of electrical systems. Here was a splendid opportunity to show St. Louis how to build a terminal.

Like St. Louis, the local railroads formed the Kansas City Terminal Railway Association. The new terminal would combine passenger operations for all the railroads and provide convenient access to local interurban rail lines and trolleys. The project also enjoyed widespread civic support, just like the St. Louis project.

But Kansas City already knew what they wanted in the way of a design; they wanted something just as wonderful as the terminals that New York was getting. So they hired Beaux Arts-trained architect Jarvis Hunt. At the time both Grand Central and the Pennsylvania Station were under construction, but Kansas City was close behind, building the third largest terminal in America.

It was a larger building than the directors first had in mind, but they were persuaded that the Kansas City area could grow to over a million people and they should plan for expansion. Once again they looked at growth in St. Louis and the effect on that terminal, now almost twenty years old. So they gave Chicago architect Jarvis Hunt a nod, and development plans were soon underway.

Kansas City's Union Station opened in 1914, just after New York's Grand Central and Pennsylvania Station terminals. The grand hall just inside the entrance was an impressive space, another Roman temple, but this one was in the heart of America.

Grand Junction, Colorado

Grand Junction's depot really is grand—one of the nicest, sturdiest buildings in the city and among the best intermediate size stations anywhere in the United States or Canada—just as it was designed to be almost ninety years ago.

The current depot replaces a pretty Queen Anne wooden structure that served the western Colorado community until about 1905, when it was torn down to make way for the new facility. As was typical of the time, the depot was designed to anticipate the needs of the future, and this part of Colorado was booming around the turn of the century, with no prospects for decline in the rapid growth of population or economic activity.

The Denver & Rio Grand railroad hired prominent architects to design its more important depots; the noted Chicago designer Henry John Schlack was commissioned for the Grand Junction project. The depot was built to last, with stone and tile throughout, and a large stained glass window above the mezzanine.

Opening day was April 17th, 1906. Three thousand people (most of the town and a lot of the local Indian population) showed up to inspect the interior that day, and everybody agreed that it was definitely the bee's knees.

As with depots across the continent, the Grand Junction building became the focus of the community many times. When Buffalo Bill and his circus came to town in a train of fifty eight cars, 10,000 locals showed up at the depot in welcome and to watch the free show, the one when all the animals were unloaded from the cars. Four presidents detrained at this building; the famous composer John Phillips Sousa, Harry Houdini, and many other public figures were received at this portal to the community.

But ten years after opening, the depot was taken over by the US government as part of the war effort. Changes were made to the building: a second floor was added to the mezzanine.

By the 1970s the roof was leaking a bit, there were electrical problems, and the Denver & Rio Grand didn't want to invest money in a building that didn't seem to have a future—except perhaps as a parking lot. Amtrak was using the structure at the time, but only as a tenant, and they elected to move a few doors down the street to a newer, more modern facility where the lights worked and the roof didn't leak.

The Leany family owns six businesses in Grand Junction and was well aware of the depot. When the building, was effectively abandoned by the railroad Jim Leany Sr. investigated the property and considered its potential. "There wasn't a crack in the structure," Jim Jr. says, "despite all the train traffic going by outside. It was obviously a very beautiful structure. The Achilles heel of the building was its roof. We realized that this building ought to be in its adolescence, not in its old age. My dad thought that if we could buy it and repair the roof properly, it ought to be good for another two hundred years, easy!"

The key to the project, as always, was money. The family decided to invest a half million dollars directly, and to raise another $700,000 from other sources. "With that kind of investment we could have one of the most beautiful buildings in Grand Junction, and one of the most historically significant," Jim explains. "We can afford to give this building back to the public, if we do it right."

The Leanys decided to acquire the building with the intention of doing a careful restoration. They started researching other depot restoration projects monitored by the National Trust for His-

Detail of New York City's Grand Central. The problem of moving large numbers of people through a structure in a timely way is part of the challenge of large depot architecture, normally solved in part by labeling every doorway with BIG letters that just about anybody can read. *Piet Halberstadt*

Grand Central was once a grand structure, a civic monument to the railroad age. That monument was dwarfed, though, by another monumental structure to a different kind of god, the immense Pan Am Building. When the demolition of Grand Central was blocked in the 1960s, one die-hard developer proposed building another huge building directly over the terminal and this charming trio of Greek mythological figures. *Piet Halberstadt*

St. Louis, Missouri. The large stained glass window sits amid this wall with its arches, windows, and incredibly detailed design work. Instead of a quick-and-dirty renovation, the project planners determined to bring the station back to its precise original 1894 glory, and they succeeded beautifully.

St. Louis, Missouri. This allegorical stained glass window spans the fifty-foot-wide entrance stairway to the grand hall; the figures represent San Francisco, St. Louis, and New York.

toric Preservation. There are about 800 such projects documented by the Trust—a wealth of data, full of successes and failures. The Trust furnished publications and guidelines to assist in the project.

"The National Trust's information is invaluable," Jim says. "They have specific publications that describe the best way to replace bricks, repoint them, seal them with modern products—somebody else has already worked out how to do it properly on an old structure like this one! Every aspect of the work we have to do—the lighting, the correct paint color, the repair of woodwork—has already been researched and all we have to do is send away for the book! And when we do the work, we will have a project supervisor who will make sure that the guidelines are being followed."

The Leany family hired an architect with previous successful restoration projects on his resume.

Living up to its name is the grand hall at the St. Louis, Missouri, depot. In part to conserve energy, certainly, public buildings are no longer designed with immense open air spaces such as this.

While studying the original construction drawings, the architect noticed that the custom tile in the list of materials was supplied by a business called the Chicago Tile Company. A little investigation revealed the company was still in business, and still had the original molds for the tiles used in the old roof. He sent some samples to the company; they matched the color and style exactly, and the roof was restored to its original condition. That's a preservation success story and is unlike many other attempts at restoration or renovation, where owners or architects simply assume that matching original materials aren't available or practical and then make compromises. A preservation professional is not only sensitive to these issues, he or she often knows of sources for authen-

Detail from the grand hall of the restored depot in St. Louis, Missouri.

tic materials that conventional building trade people would ignore.

"We're going to take out that second floor," Jim Leany says, "and we are going to take the building back to the way it looked in 1906. We are going to put the original stained glass window back in its frame, and we know where the original clock is, along with the brass 'Women's Retiring Room' and 'Men's Smoking Room' signs. Since we have the architect's original construction drawings we can put the spiral staircase back the way it was, too. We have everything we need to do a good restoration. In fact, I think the restoration will be the easy part; making the building part of a successful business that pays for itself will be harder, but we think we can do that, too."

UNION STATION

Left: The Union depot in downtown Indianapolis, Indiana, is a tribute to revival rather than disposal. The depot sits in the midst of the city's downtown area and has been restored and revitalized to become a cornerstone of civic activities from shopping to entertainment to special events.

Right: The handsome stonework of the Indianapolis depot looks elegant and proud amid downtown buildings that range from historic to ultra-modern.

Bottom: The centerpiece of the Indianapolis depot is this great hall, with its high ceiling, scores of windows, and gorgeous renovation of detail such as railings and lamps. Several restaurants line the walkway down the middle of the space, a walkway that leads visitors to a busy retail complex and one of the highlights for rail fans: a hotel whose facade incorporates the exteriors of old rail cars. A person looking out the window of a car is actually looking out the window of a hotel room. Life-sized plaster sculptures of old travelers, conductors, and porters dot the sidewalk just outside these "rooms."

Previous page top: Los Angeles Union Station was one of the last large-scale depots built in the nation, and was completed prior to World War II. During the war it served as a busy hub for armed traveling service personnel as well as civilian travelers.

Parts of the Los Angeles Union Station are open air, so it's not uncommon to see pigeons flying about overhead in the lofty sections of the building. Even so, the station is well maintained and kept clean.

There is still a lot of traffic running through the Los Angeles Union Station. It remains a hub of West Coast rail travel. The building has undergone some renovation in recent years, and it is still an impresive depot that fairly glitters in the California sun.

EAST
ELY
40

CHAPTER 6

Nevada Northern–Suspended In Time

Preserved by the Desert

A railroad depot, out of context, is just a collection of bricks or boards. The architectural style may be pretty or quaint, but these buildings don't really make much sense when they are taken away from the rails, when the trains don't stop in front of them, when they are converted into pizza parlors, gift shops, or museums. Then they cease being genuine depots—the real functions that serve passengers and locomotives are gone, the real railroad business disappears. Those buildings become ghosts of depots, and are living on in another kind of afterlife.

The dry air of Nevada preserves many things, one of which is a perfectly intact, still functional railroad, the Nevada Northern. The entire station at East Ely, Nevada, has been preserved; the passenger depot, freight depot, and the office building, the towers, maintenance shop, electrical shop, and all the other little shacks and sheds that usually make up a station. The buildings still contain all the spare parts and tools; the offices still have the calendars and memos. The line shut down suddenly in 1983, and its ghost is so vibrant and lifelike that it is easy to get a sense of what a railroad and its depots and shops could mean to people, places, and times long past.

Just getting to the Nevada Northern is an adventure. The town of Ely is about 130 miles south of Interstate 80 (from Salt Lake City go west to the town of Wells; turn left at the bordello called the Hacienda). It is a part of the world that seems almost abandoned; there are

Perhaps the best preserved complete railroad in the United States is the Nevada Northern, an intact shortline operation based in the remote town of Ely, Nevada. When the line shut down in 1983, virtually every element—locomotive, payroll record, invoice, and pin-up calendar—was left right were it was, including this nifty 1910 Baldwin locomotive. The entire kit and caboodle is now owned by the State of Nevada, and a private operation, the White Pine Historic RR, operates out of the old depot.

The tiny community of Currie, Nevada, is in one of the most remote locations in the nation. It never amounted to much but it was a crew change point and it had a depot. You could buy a ticket here, get on a train, and be in Chicago or New York within a few days, which some folks did right until 1941, when the Nevada Northern suspended passenger operations. But this little depot stayed open until 1983, its agent managing train orders and attending to a tiny freight business. The depot and this section of right-of-way is now owned by the Los Angeles Water Department, which insists the structure be moved or destroyed.

virtually no cars on the road. You can look across fifty miles of the beautiful, sparse Nevada landscape without seeing a house, a barn, a road, or a fence. Even today Ely is in the middle of the frontier, at the end of what Life magazine recently called "the loneliest road in America."

The Nevada Northern has always been a rather remarkable railroad. In an era of railroad robber barons, where railroads were hacked up to sell to the highest bidder, this unique railroad remains as a testimonial to the special efforts of rare businessmen—those who put people before profit. The Nevada Northern remains intact today because of the values and concerns of two businesses: Mark Requa and the company that first opened the Ely copper operation, and Kennecott Copper, the company that closed it.

Mark Requa was a railroad man, one of that new breed of managers who had taken over failing lines after the depression of the 1890s. He had assumed active management of Nevada's Eureka & Palisade Railroad and he was looking for regular paying customers for his little line. His scouts had spotted an enormous copper deposit, just out of reach of the Eureka & Palisade, about seventy-five miles away. Requa had a dilemma; should he extend his little line over four mountain ranges to the new deposit, or should he build a completely new railroad using an easier route. He carefully studied the alternatives. It was cheaper to build 140 miles of completely new, standard-gauge railroad than to try to upgrade the narrow-gauge Eureka & Palisade and extends its route another seventy-five miles.

Requa recognized that the copper deposits could not be profitably mined without a railroad so he reorganized his railroad and mining companies. He combined his White Pine Copper Company with

his other mining properties into the new Nevada Consolidated Copper Company, then he invited other investors. With this investment money he financed the new railroad, starting construction in the fall of 1905. Construction took a year and the line opened in September of 1906 with a three-day party that is still chronicled. Mark Requa resigned from the railroad in December of that year to concentrate on his mining interests. He was widely respected, known as an unusually scrupulous person who was careful with money. His ability to resolve tough problems and implement a course of action speaks for itself. He was regarded with special consideration and affection and had made a major contribution to the citizens of Ely and the state of Nevada. He had built and turned over a complete, profitable railroad, a critical and extremely vital asset to the regional economy.

Kennecott Copper Company first entered the life of the citizens of Ely about 1915. The company had its ups and downs in the international copper market but the Kennecott Company always took care of its workers. Mining is a tough, dangerous business, and Kennecott is a corporation with a longtime reputation for consideration. So in 1983, when it became obvious that the mining operations in the Ely area were going to be closed permanently, they did not just walk away from their railroad and the local economy. Instead they waited until an arrangement could be worked out with the citizens of the area. It took nearly ten years to put in place, but today the East Ely station, home of the Nevada Northern Railroad, is in the hands of people who care. Kennecott Copper turned over the railroad to the White Pine Historical Railroad Foundation and the State of Nevada. The Foundation operates the railroad; you can still buy a ticket at the depot and take a trip through southern Nevada. And the state of Nevada maintains the East Ely Railroad Depot Museum, probably the most intact and complete collection of mining and railroad history anywhere in the United States.

The East Ely Railroad Depot museum is a dream come true for a railroad enthusiast; it's heaven on earth for the railroad museum curator. Sean Pitts is the curator with the dream job and he enjoys telling the Nevada Northern story:

"Nevada Northern is enormously significant because it represents in microcosm what railroads did for the whole country. Here is little Ely, Nevada, a place so remote that it took two weeks to travel the 240 miles from the nearest major town, Salt Lake City, and it didn't really amount to much until the railroad arrived. Most of the "buildings" were either tents, or half-tent structures with wooden floors and canvas roofs. There had been deposits of gold and silver found nearby as early as 1858, but it was so remote that it was almost not practical to mine.

"But in 1900 a huge, commercial-grade deposit of copper ore was identified near the village. Edison's light bulb was just becoming popular and everyone in the country wanted electricity; the need for copper wire for electrical power skyrocketed. So there was a market, and there was a resource—but the only problem was that the deposit was inaccessible.

"Enter a man named Mark Requa, who had a vision—along with money and a railroad that he has received for his birthday, the Eureka & Palisade Railroad. The Eureka mines had all paid out, and the little railroad wasn't making any money; he believed the White Mine copper deposit represented an opportunity to make his railroad profitable.

"Seventy-five miles of Nevada desert separated the Eureka line from Ely. Requa chose a route for the extension that was twice as long but on level ground. He built a new railroad up to the Southern

The Nevada Northern never needed a roundhouse but made do with an engine house and associated shops, and this is the blacksmith shop. It might not look like much but it is, in its way, part of the wonder of Nevada Northern: inside it is exactly as it was when the line was in operation, complete with old girlie calendars, tools, coke for the furnace, and a few half-finished projects lying about where they were left the day the line shut down. Few of these buildings survive anywhere, but here is perhaps the very last of the breed, complete and in context. If you are lucky you can peek through the window and see it all, including the ghosts of the railroad blacksmiths long departed.

On his first day at work as curator for the Nevada Northern, Sean Pitts was approached by an old man with a crumpled piece of paper. On the paper were the combinations for all the safes on the railroad. Inside one big safe in the depot Sean found all the records of the line, silver buttons for the dining car attendants, and a pin-up calendar from the 1940s. This smaller safe in the freight house hasn't been opened yet—he's been busy with other discoveries, but he's planning to look inside one of these days.

Pacific main line, north of Ely, at a place called Cobre (CO-bray), the Spanish word for copper. Construction began in 1905; by July 4th of 1906, the line had reached Cherry Creek. On the 29th of September, the rails finally reached Ely. The citizens of Ely recognized the significance of this event, and celebrated with the biggest party in the town's history. This little town was now, for the first time, linked to the rest of the world. For someone from a big city that might not seem like such a big deal, but people in Ely suddenly had the option of travel to the rest of the world, for the first time ever."

An Affair to Remember

The party began on the 29th of September, 1906. A train load of dignitaries arrived; the governor of the state of Nevada, senators, industrialists, civic leaders from Utah and points east. The result is a huge, drunken party that lasted for three days. A small herd of cattle was barbecued and thousands of people attended. Some of the people at the party had never seen a train in their entire lives—and it scared the hell out of them. Steam engines are large and dark; they sound as if they are breathing. The Native American population cleared the area.

One of the notable, but not very dignified personages was a woman called Kerosene Kate, the town's leading prostitute, a woman who helped pioneer her special industry in Ely. Kate is described in legend and lore as being "frail, fat, and forty." Having consumed her share and perhaps a little more of the free-flowing liquor, she had adjourned to the ladies outhouse situated alongside the new depot. While attending to business, the whistle of the locomotive nearby was sounded. This apparently startled Kate, who promptly became stuck. The services of four strong men were required to extract Ely's most precious asset, a circumstance that became the highlight of the entire event and Kate's moment in history.

Back to Business

After three days of foolishness, Ely's party was over, and everybody went back to work. The Ely copper smelter is the world's largest with an initial capacity of producing eight tons of concentrate per day in 1908. Within two years that doubled, and, by 1918, the smelter was producing thirty-two tons of copper concentrate every day. Producing the copper was relatively easy; the railroad was the key to making the business profitable by getting the product to market.

The town of Ely quickly became very prosperous. People were making excellent wages. Copper went out on the railroad, all sorts of manufactured goods started coming in. After 1906 it became possible to have in your home anything that might be found in the finest homes in Chicago or San Francisco, thanks to the railroad and the Sears and Montgomery Ward catalogues. Ely started to become a city instead of a village. A year after the rails arrived the Northern Hotel was built—"the finest hotel between Reno and Salt Lake," according to Ely's residents. Then the Nevada Hotel was built in 1910, and an urban skyline began to form.

The original depot was built right in the middle of downtown Ely, about a block from the town square. Fifty-seven trains a day thundered up and down the main street. The merchants of the town appreciated the increased prosperity the railroad produced—but the noise, soot, embers, and disruption were major problems. "You're ruining our business," they complained, despite the fact that the railroad had actually accomplished the opposite. The merchants' association asked the railroad to move the tracks and the depot. The railroad responded, in effect, "go to hell."

The depot at East Ely served many functions, including the offices for the railroad management. Depots often did double duty of this sort, but when this depot was abandoned in 1983, all the paperwork, office equipment, and furniture was left in place, a kind of time capsule.

The merchants took the railroad to court—and won! The depot and tracks were ordered removed from the city streets. In spite, the railroad decided to build its own town, complete with depot, stores, shops, bank, post office, and other civil amenities at a site to the east, well away from the town of Ely proper. Now, instead of one town out in the middle of nowhere, there were two—Ely and East Ely. The two communities remained separated until 1974, with separate post offices, governments, and identities, three miles apart in the Nevada desert. Today motels, restaurants, and a few neighborhoods have filled in the space between the two towns, affecting what seems like a reconciliation.

Currie

When the line was planned, right-of-way was acquired up the Steptoe Valley, a place where your closest neighbor might be ten miles away. There wasn't much difficulty getting the ranchers to sign on the dotted line, but one of them, a man named Grant, added a proviso to the contract: every time the train passed through it had to sound the whistle! Grant loved the idea of the railroad and was delighted with the trains coming and going past the ranch. For the first time, his ranch was linked to the outside world.

A tiny station was built at the halfway point between Ely and the Southern Pacific mainline up at

The cockpit of old No. 40 is pretty Spartan by modern standards, but it still gets the job done after eighty-five-plus years. When the Nevada Northern was resurrected in 1991, the Baldwin was still in operable condition, in spite of being "rode hard and put up wet." The tender for the engine was a different story; the water tank was left full and the rust had to be removed, but the whole thing was put back on track quite quickly.

Next page: They fire up No. 40 on weekends and make up a little mixed "consist" for a little trip around the old right-of-way. The Nevada Northern even offers driving lessons for aspiring engineers for a fee.

Cobre, a little depot at the Currie ranch, and a primitive hotel alongside. This little depot was typical of the smallest, most unpretentious rural stations—a place where the rare passenger could board the occasional train. The depot served passengers until 1941, when the service stopped, and then it housed the local agent until the line closed in 1983. It is still there, alongside the tracks, dehydrated but intact.

Center of the Nevada Northern Universe

When the new town of East Ely was planned, its focus and anchor was the new depot at 1100 Avenue A. All the other buildings at the station were placed around the site of the new depot building. The depot was begun in 1906 and finished the next year, constructed of sandstone and finished with stucco. The railroad administrators decided that they weren't going to build just a depot, but a grand depot—every detail was designed to connote permanence and legitimacy, particularly to the burgers of old Ely, who, it was felt, had kicked the Nevada Northern out of the very town it had built. They found Frederick Hale, an architect/builder with a

40

background in mining engineering to design a good, solid structure. Hale came up with a good, solid, sturdy, and commodious design, up-to-date but not too fancy. The new East Ely depot was built in the mission revival style, which was a very popular style at the turn of the century.

Building stone isn't common in Nevada, but the engineers discovered a source for suitable material about seventy miles up the line, where the tracks went through the Currie ranch. The rock was quarried, loaded, and shipped back to the new town site on flatcars. The new depot was the largest, grandest building in the whole county for many years. No expense (as they say) was spared in the construction of this depot. The paneling, fixtures, and details were all of the very finest quality available. The furniture was state-of-the-art and top-of-the-line. The wooden freight depot building was built a little distance away from the elegant depot building.

The Nevada Northern operated its business office out of the second floor of the depot for its entire corporate life. The superintendent and railroad officers all conducted their business upstairs; the passengers bought tickets and waited on the first floor. The payroll was paid from here. The telegraph office was here, too, for the entire line, from the terminus on the Southern Pacific main line at Cobre on the north to Kimberly in the west. The depot was the center of the Nevada Northern universe for the life of the line. The station itself includes forty-nine buildings, housing all of the functions necessary to maintain and operate a complete railroad. It included a steam power plant to heat the depot and offices.

But the real purpose of the line was to haul copper ore to the concentrator for refining, and to carry the heavy ingots of copper away to market. Passenger traffic was a sideline, just as it was with most railroads from the very beginning.

Passenger traffic, though, was a brisk sideline during those first years. The Southern Pacific transcontinental trains stopped at the little depot up at Cobre every day (except Sunday), disgorging flocks of passengers intent on visiting the boom town of Ely. A little Baldwin locomotive in Nevada Northern livery stood by to meet them, then transported the visitors in high style to the little twin cities to the south.

The train carried mining engineers, technicians, simple miners, preachers, traveling salesmen, prostitutes, Women's Christian Temperance Union activists, clerks, Indians, U.S. marshals, prisoners, and mail-order brides. In the baggage and freight cars were caskets, pianos, ore crushers, dresses in the lat-

Previous page: The 4-6-0 Baldwin didn't really need to be restored to be used, although the brass got polished and the boiler needed re-certification.

The scale in the freight depot still works, and the stamps to mark packages and crates still wait to be used. The graffiti on the wall is a railroad depot tradition; everyone who works in the freight depot is expected to leave his mark on the wall with all the others. Some depot restoration projects paint over these marks but they are evidence of the time when these places were alive with very human beings and the commerce of a community.

est fashions, ammunition in dozens of calibers, dynamite by the carload, and medicines guaranteed to cure gout, cancer, and syphilis. The train brought fresh fruit and vegetables from far-away places, along with canned goods, meat, and poultry in tremendous variety and at lower cost. The train brought children to school in the morning and took them home in the afternoon. Newspapers from Chicago and even New York arrived only a few days late, along with the mail with its checks, bills, postcards, glad tidings, and funeral notices from people far away.

But the number of passengers waiting to transfer from the Southern Pacific to the Ely train at Cobre started slacking off in the 1930s; the Depression hit every business, and the Nevada Northern was no exception. As the economy improved though, the passenger traffic never fully recovered. People owned cars now, and that deflected some of the traffic. Buses replaced the stage coach, too, and some of the passenger traffic was siphoned off by this mode of travel as well. Finally, in 1941, the last scheduled passenger train made its final run up to Cobre and back, and that was the end of passenger service on the Nevada Northern.

The depots still had plenty of work to do, though, even the little ones at Currie and Cherry Creek. There was still plenty of copper concentrate to ship off to the east, and there was still plenty of freight business for the line. The stationmasters at the remote little depots continued to issue train orders and work the signals, even if they didn't sell tickets any more. And that's the way Nevada Northern conducted business for another forty years.

The people who worked in the mines didn't notice the trend right away, but the mine owners and operators knew the whole operation was in trouble in the late 1970s. First, there was a worldwide shortage of copper that drove the price of the commodity up; then foreign producers from Peru and elsewhere got into the business in a large way, and the price for the metal dropped off the scale. American producers had

Above: In the big safe inside the depot, Sean Pitts discovered the payroll books going back to the beginning of the railroad. The names, dates, and figures help tell the story of the time, place, and people who once worked in and around this old depot.

The carpenter shop used to repair components of the cars and the depot, too. Every railroad maintained shops like this one, normally adjacent to a roundhouse.

never really bothered to modernize or make the operation much more efficient than it had been back in 1910. Suddenly, the Ely operation was no longer competitive on the world market.

The End of the Line—1983

Ely's residents ought to have seen it coming, but they didn't; when the mine shut down in 1979, they ought to have realized something was amiss. Sean Pitts, the Nevada state historian, says "I've done oral history interviews with residents, and I said, 'surely you must have known that the railroad was going to shut down, that the smelter was going to shut down—the mine was already shut down. The paper was reporting that copper was being produced in Peru far cheaper than it was here! Surely you knew that the union was getting such a large chunk of the profits that there wasn't anything left for modernization.'

"The woman told me, 'oh, no, we were good Christian people. The company always took care of us!' And that's the way many people in Ely felt about it; they just didn't want to see it coming. It is my suspicion that a lot of people could see it coming, but just didn't want to believe it and ignored what was obviously happening. It was the only way of life they had ever known. There was a job waiting for every kid that finished high school, and a scholarship for every kid that wanted to go to college. The work was relatively dangerous, but it paid very well. For generations of people here, the company was the entire known universe. The company floated loans to the city, underwrote Little League, subsidized cultural events for the community—everything!"

The layoff was announced in 1983. Nobody was surprised or alarmed; there had been a layoff every three years, whenever the union and the company were renegotiating their contract. Since layoffs were a part of the normal routine, the Nevada Northern employees all assumed they'd be back in three days, or three weeks—three months at the most—and they just got up and left at the end of the day. The calendars are still open to that day, work schedules are still on the bulletin boards. The people walked out of the building at the end of that

OFFICE

final day, locked the doors and went home to wait for the call to return to work. While they waited, the company finished the formalities and went out of business.

"The residents of Ely were stunned," says Sean. "Even during the Depression of the 1930s the company cut way back, and people worked only two or three days a week instead of five, but everybody worked. The company had never closed!"

But Nevada Northern did close down, tight. The whole operation was left just where it was on that last day. The State of Nevada finally acquired part of the facilities and hired Sean Pitts as State Curator with the mission to preserve, protect, and defend this resource.

"My first day of work was April 27th, 1992," Sean says. "I thought, Where do you begin? So I started by vacuuming the floors and general clean-up. While I was busy with this I heard the front door open and someone coming upstairs. It was an older gentleman, and he asked if I was the curator and demanded to know what I was going to do with it all. I tried to tell him of my grand vision—about the exhibits, the collections, about all the things we could teach visitors. After about three minutes of my spiel, he interrupts and says, 'Good enough for me; here!'

"He handed me a crumpled up little piece of paper with numbers on it. It didn't mean anything to me. Then the man said, 'When I retired from the railroad in 1983 I wasn't real happy with the settlement; I had access to the combinations of the vaults, so I took them with me—and here they are.'

"'You're kidding,' I told him. 'You mean these vaults haven't been opened since the railroad shut down?'

"'C'mere young feller, and I'll show ya,' he says. He opened the first vault, and I will never forget the feeling of breathing nine-year-old air! It was one of the most incredible, wonderful things for someone in my business. I was surrounded by documents and artifacts from the early part of the 20th century—locked away for all these years. I was euphoric!

"'Do you know what's in here?' I asked him.

"'No. I figured that if it was important enough for the company to lock up, it was important enough to keep locked up.'"

In the vaults Sean found the payroll ledgers going all the way back to the beginning. There were

Above: One result of the web of rails that covered the country was the invention of the traveling salesman, a breed of riffraff admonished by this sign to avoid the premises. In fact a lot of folks found that rail travel improved business, including prostitutes, who liked to move from one town to another every few months, normally by rail, and often to the wild, wide open town of Ely, where they still conduct business in the town's red light district alongside the tracks.

Previous page: These tourists are boarding an excursion train at the depot in East Ely for a few hours aboard the Nevada Northern. It is hard to appreciate today how much a difference this building and the tracks in front of it made to the lives of people back in the early 1900s, but it was an immense, radical development at the time. Before the train, a trip to Salt Lake City or Reno, the nearest major towns, could take two weeks or more; afterwards, by train, a day or less.

The Nevada Northern depot at East Ely was built with all the best that money could buy, including tons of stone quarried especially for the structure.

The Currie Hotel isn't on the AAA recommended list but there were times when it was an important, welcome oasis in the desert for a hot, dry, tired mining engineer or rancher. In fact, hotels like this one sprouted up alongside depots whenever the rails went in, the beginnings of a settlement, a community, a town, and ultimately a city.

boxes of silver buttons, still in new condition, for the uniforms of dining car attendants—who haven't served a meal on the Nevada Northern since 1941. A pinup calendar from the 1950s is still on the wall of one of the vaults. There was every document, record, and detail to tell the story of the depot, the people, the rolling stock, and every element of the Nevada Northern railroad.

The depot is open and operating again, and not much has changed. Nothing has been renovated or restored; nothing needed to be restored. It was all just waiting for the right company to come back and start up again. You can buy a ticket, get on the same old train powered by the original 1910 Baldwin and take a ride. You can't, at this writing, go up to Cobre, but you can ride around a sizable portion of Nevada. And when the train comes back through Ely, past the red light district (where the business of pleasure is still quite legal), the prostitutes from the three bordellos still come out in their flimsy attire to wave at the passengers and train crew, exhibiting their wares pretty much like Kerosene Kate probably did back when the line began. They wave, the passengers wave back, and the engineer whistles a friendly salute. In Nevada some things never change.

So young Sean Pitts, custodian for the State of Nevada, essentially inherited a whole railroad, intact but a bit dusty, with all the records, office supplies, spare parts, rolling stock, locomotives, and depots, all in pristine condition. And he didn't even have to pry open the safes to discover that nothing had been looted. It was as if the people of Ely (and East Ely) had all figured that, sooner or later, the railroad would come back and start operating again... and in a way, it did.

The depot at East Ely was designed to be the center of a railroad and a whole town, designed explicitly that way by the Nevada Northern. The building contained the passenger depot, ticket office, waiting room, telegraph office, and general offices for the line until 1983.

Depots at larger towns usually split the passenger and the freight business into two operations, each with their own building. The Nevada Northern freight house is a long wooden building with space allocated for each of the major local customers inside, each with its own door.

Left: There are few coal plants still around, but this is one. Fodder for the iron horse had to be imported long distances and in large quantities, then stored in strategic locations.

Top: The water tower is another survivor of the Nevada Northern depot complex. Many depots were adjacent to structures like this in the days of steam.

4509 4509
354

Roundhouses and Shops

The Roundhouse

The roundhouse is a very special and wonderful type of American building, associated only with railroads. They are a special sort of garage for locomotives, and their characteristic shape makes them easily recognizable. But the function of the roundhouse, while perfect for the care and feeding of the iron horse, produced a form of structure that doesn't adapt well to other uses. The unfortunate result is that a very small percentage of roundhouses have survived, a much smaller proportion than the survival rate for depots.

Who designed the first roundhouse? It was probably a development rather than a design. And like most other railroad technology, it probably developed initially in the mining districts of England.

The Stable for the Iron Horse

Depots and roundhouses were two essential elements of a functioning railroad, but the two kinds of structures have met two very different fates. Depots have been mostly preserved and protected but the roundhouses have nearly all been destroyed. But what is a roundhouse, anyway?

Well, the roundhouse was the perfect solution for a lot of problems associated with the steam locomotive. It's the stable for the iron horse, that wonderful snorting, steaming, and seemingly tireless steed. Consuming huge quantities of coal and belching fire, this magnificent creature required careful grooming in order to perform properly, and the place that grooming was done was a building designed expressly for the task.

Grand Island, Nebraska. This lovely old engine house was part the first big shop complex built by the Union Pacific on its march westward toward Promintory in the 1860s. Recently acquired by the Nebraska Central, a new short-line operation, the building is in spotless condition and ready to service a new breed of locomotives.

Engineer Joe Siemons backs No. 28 out of the Sierra RR roundhouse at Jamestown, California, for another day of tourist excursion rides. *Mike Halberstadt*

Like the stagecoaches they replaced, locomotives had to be fed and watered every 30 miles or so, to maintain boiler pressure and operating strength. When loads were heavy or the hills were steep, the horses needed more fuel. And "helper" horses, or in this case, engines, were stabled along the route at strategically placed sidings so they could quickly be added to either the front or rear of a train as needed. It is not surprising then, to find early locomotive maintenance sheds and depots, located along the lines at about the same frequency as the stagecoaches they replaced, about every thirty miles. Located at terminal or division yards, these structures followed two basic shapes, a square shed "engine house" or the circular type we now refer to as a "roundhouse."

Both types of buildings had advantages, and both had serious drawbacks. Remember that locomotives cannot turn around; at some point the engine had to be pointed toward its destination with its "consist" coupled on behind. There are two ways to turn a locomotive around: a transfer-table and a turntable.

So the choice of train shed, round or square, depended on how much flat space you had available for your trackage. A square shed with a transfer table some distance away from the building was in some ways the most efficient. Several engines could be run out, one behind the other, in case of fire or when engines were needed in a hurry. The shed could be fairly small, but the track approach took a fair amount of space.

On the other hand, a round-house allowed a lot more engines to be housed under cover, but there would be a tremendous bottleneck in case of fire—and fire was a common hazard, as we'll discuss later. A roundhouse covered more square footage under the roof, but only really needed one track for access. There were some other advantages to a roundhouse in those days before electrical lighting. The engine could be placed in the best light available for the maintenance crew. A roundhouse had good natural light from windows all around the perimeter, so repairs could be made more efficiently.

Roundhouse Design

Roundhouses are tricky to design. They're expensive, consume a lot of real estate, and if planned badly, tend to catch fire, become too small for your engines, or fail in other ways.

Pretend that you own a railroad and are making plans for a new roundhouse. The design process begins with a look deep into the crystal ball—what does the future hold for your railroad? How many engines will need service? How big will they be? The turntable must be at least as large as the biggest locomotive you expect to ever own, and as the (Delaware and Hudson) learned, even 105 feet wasn't big enough when the Challenger series of locomotives was introduced in the 1930s.

Since the hazard of fire is so great in a roundhouse, with all its flammable oils, paints, solvents, and fuel (coal or diesel), some provision ought to be made to protect the expensive engines when the inevitable finally happens. One such provision included early was the placement of water barrels and fire buckets throughout the structure, even on the roof. Another was the inclusion of sprinkler systems. Yet another was the common practice of making the roundhouse big enough that enough trackage existed between the turntable and the front of the roundhouse to permit the engine and tender to be rolled outside if and when a fire occurred. And one way to facilitate getting the engine out of the building was to slope the tracks away from the building just enough to make it possible for a few men to push a cold, dead engine out of danger.

Inside, drop pits were usually included for some or all the stalls; these made it easier to pull a wheel. Skylights provided light, and flues ducted most of the smoke out of the building.

The stalls, along with the turntable, had to be long enough to fully accommodate the longest engine, otherwise you couldn't close the doors—a serious problem if your roundhouse happens to be in North Dakota on a stormy January night.

Ventilation was also important, particularly on a torrid August afternoon in Georgia. Even before the days of air conditioning, roundhouses had forced airflow and well-planned ventilation.

Water was an important consideration in the days of steam; tremendous quantities were needed for boiler cleaning, the locomotive wash rack, and to fill the tender's boiler feed tanks. Stationary steam engines provided power before electricity took over, and these engines, too, required clean water with a minimum mineral content.

How big should your roundhouse be? There are two ways to measure size: diameter and number of stalls. American roundhouses tended to be larger than European roundhouses because engines tended to be longer. The diameter of a roundhouse depended on the length of the engine that needed to fit on the turntable. In a growing railroad, turntables were made longer than needed in order to accommodate the possibility of acquiring larger, longer engines in the future.

Oneonta Roundhouse

As an example, the Delaware and Hudson Railroad started out with an eleven-stall roundhouse in Oneonta, New York, in 1870 to shelter its little fleet of thirty-five engines. It was a sturdy structure, built of quarried stone, brick, and massive timbers. Each engine bay tapered from thirteen feet at the door to twenty-five feet at the back wall, with sixty-five feet of track under cover, all served by a sixty foot manual turntable out front. No sooner was it finished than the company began work on doubling the structure, adding another eleven stalls. Two years later, though, the enlargement was still incomplete, and the D&H put it on hold while three other shop buildings were constructed, including a foundry, an

Heavy, hand-wrought iron hooks hold the Sierra RR roundhouse doors open. This one was probably made in the blacksmith shop nearby, within the railroad shop complex, in 1897 when the place was built.

No. 28 is oil-fired; Joe arrives at the roundhouse about sunrise to light the boiler. It takes hours for the engine to get up steam, and while it starts to simmer, Joe scurries around the locomotive, inspecting, oiling, and monitoring the gradual increase in pressure. *Mike Halberstadt*

engine repair facility, and another roundhouse. Then the first roundhouse was finally finished in 1876.

By 1881 the D&H was running out of room for its growing collection of motive power units and began planning yet another roundhouse, just to the north of the original structure. The basic dimensions of the new building were identical to the original but with a larger turntable. After just five months of construction the new roundhouse was completed and opened for business in January of 1882.

By 1900 the D&H owned 165 locomotives, many far too big to fit completely inside the old engine houses—even after several stalls were extended. By 1905 the senior management of the company decided to build yet another roundhouse. This time, though, the company decided to plan for the future; the result was going to be the biggest roundhouse in the world, designed for the biggest locomotives then available or on the drawing board.

The new roundhouse design included fifty-two stalls, each one measuring 80 feet long, and a massive, electrically powered 75-foot turntable. The building was to be over 400 feet across, constructed of fireproof materials. Nearly two miles of track were used within the roundhouse to service all the stalls, with one track aperture for locomotives leaving the facility and two tracks for inbound engines. It was one of the wonders of the age.

The D&H architects had thought of everything! Inbound engines dumped their ashes directly into waiting gondola cars in a cleverly designed ashpit. High-pressure pumps delivered water to eight 2-inch hose connections at the wash rack. The roundhouse itself was built largely of concrete, with careful attention to every detail. Massive skylights provided illumination, and a heating plant furnished forced hot air into the entire building during the arctic New York winters. Special vents ducted away the smoke from engines inside the building, keeping the air inside reasonably healthy.

The facility opened in 1906 to rave reviews in the railroad press. Large numbers of new people moved to Oneonta, such as shop workers and their families, swelling the population of the little town by more than a third.

The whole shop complex became a beehive of carefully orchestrated activity, twenty-four hours a day, seven days a week. Engines arrived at the complex for scheduled maintenance or for emergency repairs. As the locomotives approached the big roundhouse, the tenders received fresh coal, water, and dried sand from bins and tanks at trackside, dumped their cinders in the ashpit, directly into waiting gondola cars. Hostlers shuttled the engines into bays around the clock while hordes of shop laborers attended to each, then sent the renovated engines back to duty up and down the line.

By 1916 even the 80-foot-long bays were becoming too small for the huge locomotives entering service, and work began on extending twenty-seven stalls to 100 feet in length. The turntable, once considered over-generous, also cramped the style of the massive engines of the day; it was lengthened to 105-feet in 1923. Even that turned out to be too small for the Challenger series of locomotives and tenders that came along in the next decade, so the D&H roundhouse crews had to split the engine and tender, moving them into the building individually.

But the big engines, the decline of the D & H's traffic, and then the transition to diesel power after World War II all combined to destroy the functions of the big roundhouse. The D & H started nibbling away at the structure, and gradually the huge build-

ing was demolished; nothing remains today on the site at Oneonta except some concrete foundations, ciders, and ghosts.

With this Oneonta "plan-ahead" lesson to learn from, now that you've got your turntable sized, add at least another engine-length between the edge of the turntable and the doors of the shed. That's because you will want to be able to run an engine out and have it wait its turn at the edge of the turntable. You will want your roundhouse to be at least an engine-length in depth in order to pull your entire locomotive inside and close the door. Engines are able to withstand bad weather, but the maintenance crew needs a fairly comfortable environment. Even with the doors closed it's tough on the crew that needs to wash a boiler in the middle of a rough northern winter!

What materials should you use for your roundhouse? Something fireproof is always preferred—brick, stone, and sheet iron have always been the materials of choice, although some lines have used wood. Stone works well, and so does brick. If you're railroad is small and not very wealthy you might consider corrugated iron. And if you cannot afford any of these, or you are building your maintenance facility in an area where these materials are limited or not available, if wood is a necessity, then consider building several small sheds, well away from each other. Losing all your motive power in a fire could be ruinous—and that was something that happened fairly frequently.

Take care that your turntable pit is covered in case of snow. If your snowfall is light, the table can usually be operated without difficulty. But in heavy snowfall you will need to shovel out the pit before rotating the turntable and your operating schedule may suffer.

Be sure and vent each of your engine stalls. It takes a day or so to get a boiler going and about four hours to get enough steam in the boiler to drive it out of the garage. All of those fumes are extremely poisonous, so provide good vents over each stack. And you will want good drainage from all of your engine pits; so if you can provide a direct drain to

The Sierra RR roundhouse was built in 1897, burned, and was rebuilt shortly thereafter. Typical of some shortline operations, the roundhouse includes the machine shop, the peaked-roof building just across the turn table.

Attention, rail fans, this is a nearly unique sight: one of the few roundhouses with a sign of its own. This is the 1888 San Jose, California, Lenzen Street roundhouse.

the sewer it will handle all of the residue more efficiently.

Shops

Shops included a number of buildings, each with its own function, its own tools, and its own crew of highly skilled personnel. The machine shop contained huge lathes, a forge for heating and bending, equipment to replace rivets, and cast replacement parts.

The carpenter's shop could rebuild an entire boxcar, replace the sides of a cattle car, or rebuild a seat in a passenger coach. The boilermakers were a special group, responsible for maintaining, repairing and testing the locomotive boilers.

Grooming the Iron Horse

It took a lot of people like Susie Torres to keep the old locomotives running, and the Southern Pacific roundhouse was full of them, from 1910, when it was built, until 1990, when it was abandoned. Railroads were frequently the largest employers in a community, making the railroad payroll the most important part of a local economy.

Part of the reason for that was the steam locomotive itself, a machine that required frequent maintenance. Shop and roundhouse workers accounted for about a quarter of all the employees working for Santa Fe around the turn of the century. Major repairs and overhauls on the Santa Fe went back to Topeka, Kansas, where over a thousand men were employed in the company shop complex. Some of these people were well-trained craftsmen: boilermakers, machinists, sheet metal fabricators, painters, carpenters, blacksmiths, pipefitters. They were assisted by platoons of unskilled or semi-skilled laborers: wipers, oilers, ash-pit men, hostlers (parking lot attendants for locomotives).

These same skills were present in most of the hundreds of roundhouses up and down the line. In fact there was at least one roundhouse for every division of every railroad, and roundhouses at many other locations as well, each intended to shelter the locomotives and the people who kept them running.

Among the most essential of these crafts were the boilermakers, a dirty, dangerous job. Steam engines use dozens of steel tubes to expose a large surface area of water to the heat of the fire in the firebox. These tubes sometimes crack, plug, or fail—occasionally with fatal consequences. Boiler explosions were fairly common a hundred years ago, and the newspapers of the time gleefully reported on the gruesome effects of high-pressure steam. So great care and attention was given this part of the engine, and considerable respect for the men who labored in the dark recesses of a cold firebox, cleaning out or replacing defective tubes. Boilermakers earned $2.94 per ten-hour day in 1874 and worked a six-day week. (All the pay data is from "Men of the Steel Rails," Drucker, p. 112.)

Machinists were also revered craftsmen, sometimes with their own specialized shop facility adjacent to the roundhouse, sometimes working in an annex within the roundhouse itself. These men performed a kind of "voodoo science" during a time when few people had experience with machinery of any kind. They knew how to disassemble, adjust, repair, and reassemble the components of the steam engine itself. Some of these machinists used the massive lathes that trued the driving wheels of the locomotive; others could fabricate or repair wheel bearings, pistons, valves, shafts, cams, and pushrods—working to tolerances of a few thousandths of an inch on a component that might be five feet across and weigh thousands of pounds. To the many illiterate and unsophisticated people in the shop these skills were akin to magic. A Santa Fe machinist earned $3.02 a day in 1874, twice what a shop la-

The Lenzen Street roundhouse in San Jose. Since its abandonment by Southern Pacific a few years ago the four remaining stalls have been taken over by transients, hoboes, and derelicts who come here to drink and camp at night. Two are leaving for lunch at the Rescue Mission across the tracks, but they'll be back later—there are still a few windows that haven't been broken, and there is still some room on the walls for more graffiti.

It's a full house at the Dakota, Minnesota & Eastern's shop in Huron, South Dakota, and these big diesels barely fit.

borer received and nearly as much as the highest paid employees, the engineers who were paid $3.35.

Shop Laborers

Hostlers and wipers were the most numerous workers in and around the roundhouse; they were semiskilled workers who only received $1.66 per day. Hostlers moved the engines in the shop complex, insured that they were fueled and watered, and operated the turntable and switches. Wipers cleaned the locomotives, sometimes using a wash rack and high-pressure hose, other times, as the title implies, using rags to remove mud and grime.

Wages actually declined for many railroad employees during the 1880s, and stayed low for many decades. Frank Fatta, a shop worker for the D&H from 1917 until 1942, started at forty-nine cents an hour and was earning $1.10 an hour when he retired in '42—as the highest salaried man in the roundhouse! That rate of pay was less than half of what a boilermaker earned sixty years previously.

Despite the low pay, the hostler's job required intelligence and alertness. As an example, one engine brought to the Oneonta, New York, roundhouse had a defective throttle—unknown to the hostler who drove it into the complex and parked it. While unattended, the locomotive started to move toward the turntable, with no one in the cab. Another hostler realized what was happening, quickly turned the table to the tracks of the wayward engine, and the locomotive picked up speed. After zooming across the turntable, the engine crashed through the roundhouse, out the back wall. While the damage was bad enough, had the locomotive crashed into the turntable the whole complex would have been out of action, a far worse possibility.

In the early years of American railroading turntables became a standard fixture in front of roundhouses. The first were entirely manual—one man could rotate the device quite easily as long as the load was balanced. But with the advent of larger and heavier engines, steam and electrical motors replaced some of the "Armstrong" platforms.

Boiler Tube Replacement

Shop laborers might be assigned to dozens of tasks, some requiring skill, others mere drudgery. One common task of the roundhouse crew was the monthly cleaning of the boiler, a wash-down with a high pressure hose. Another, performed by the boilermaker and the boilermaker's helper, involved cleaning each tube with a special reamer on the end of a long rod; these same men replaced the

There's at least one real roundhouse in America still doing the work it was designed to do, full time: the Dakota, Minnesota & Eastern at Huron, South Dakota. The stalls are full of modern diesels and the turntable was getting a workout the day this photograph was made.

Nevada Northern's engine house is still full of engines, but the windows are falling out of their frames. The facility is now owned by the state of Nevada and is gradually getting caught up on some of the maintenance that was deferred during the nine years the line was shut down.

tubes by laboriously chiseling off the lip on one end, then driving the tube out; a new tube was then installed and locked into place by beading the ends into tight flanges.

Working Conditions

Normal working hours for roundhouse employees were for ten hours a day, six days a week, but at peak traffic periods some people worked seventy-five hour weeks and more. Sundays were normally a day of rest for most of the shopmen, but not all, and not at peak periods.

The shops were hot in the summer, cold in the winter, and the light was sometimes dim. It was a dangerous place, in several ways. You could fall in one of the pits, get burned by the steam, slip on the greasy floor, and be crushed when one of the massive wheels toppled over. But there was another hazard; the smoke and fumes that filled the atmosphere of the place. Train work was (and still is) dangerous work.

Party Time

Despite the dirt and the danger, working in the big roundhouses was rewarding in many ways. Susie Torres stayed on partly for the money, which was

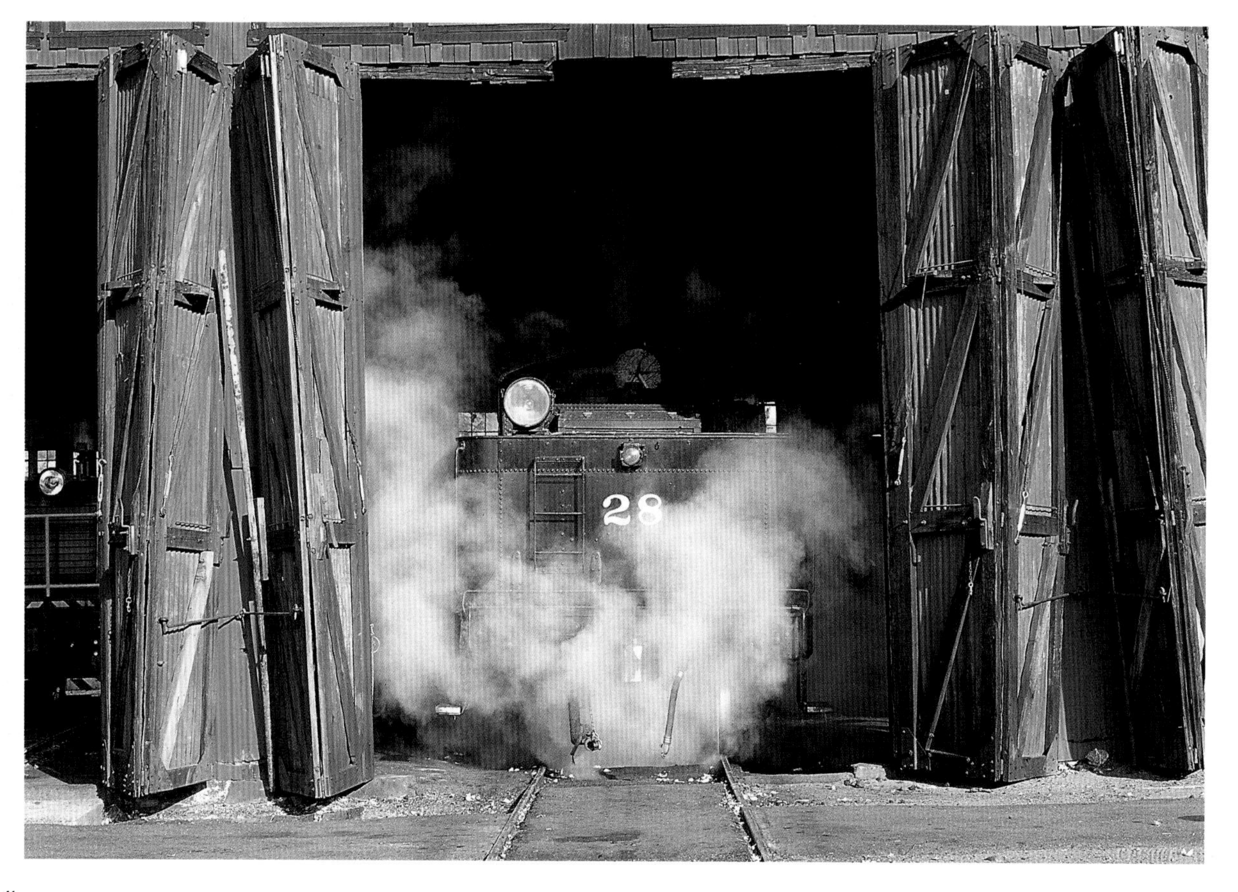

After warming up for a few hours, the oil-fired Baldwin is ready for duty for the Sierra RR, Jamestown, California, on a cold winter moring.

Red worked on this engine when it was in passenger service during the late 1940s and he helped bring it back to life fifty years later.

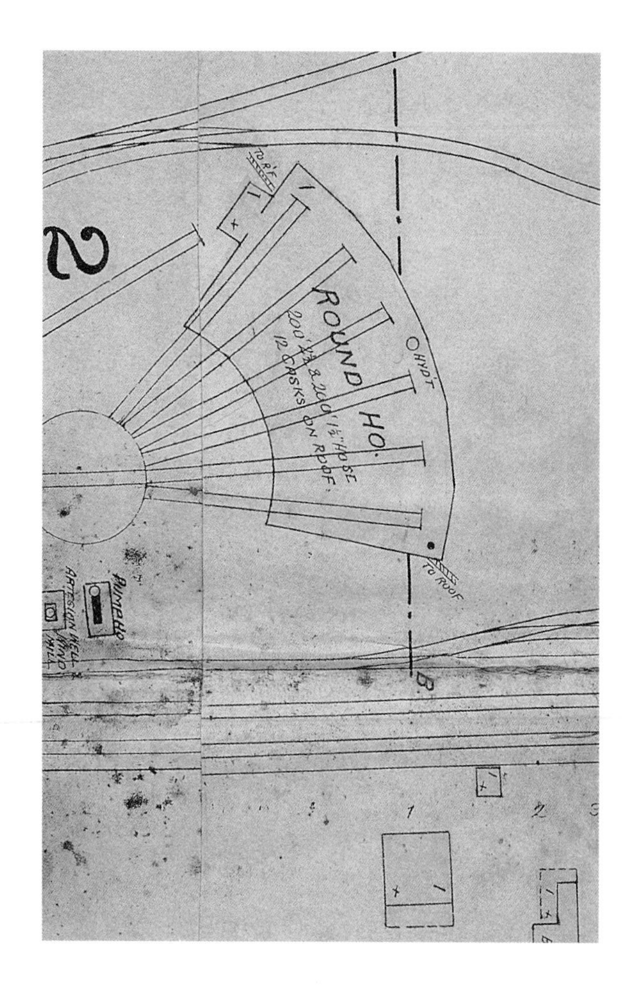

A Sanborn insurance map from around 1890 shows a small roundhouse and turntable (since demolished) at San Jose, California. Roundhouses were notorious fire hazards and frequently burned down, sometimes taking whole neighborhoods with them. This map indicated fire mains and water sources nearby. *Franklin Maggi Collection*

good for the time, and partly for the sociable pleasures that developed within rail communities, especially roundhouse communities.

Southern Pacific, along with other roads, was quite generous with its shop staff. Friday barbecues were a tradition at the South San Francisco shop complex, as they were at many other division roundhouses. The bigger shops often had orchestras and provided concerts on a regular schedule, on company time. Shop workers were treated to festive excursions, too, aboard a train made up for the occasion, filled with Southern Pacific employees and their families.

Going, going, gone

Shops and roundhouses, yards and maintenance facilities brought a tremendous payroll into a tiny town. The location of a major division yard in your town was highly desirable. Grand Island, Nebraska, was the location of the first maintenance point for

From Roundhouse to Hobo Camp

Our old Southern Pacific roundhouse over on Lenzen street here in San Jose still stands, one of just a half-dozen survivors left in all of California. Its brick walls are gradually collapsing, the weight of the years pushing and pulling at the old building. It has only been empty for a couple of years, ever since the locomotive service facility was shifted to a bigger yard about fifty miles away.

The pits between the tracks, designed to allow mechanics to crawl under the big steam locomotives of 1910 are now filled with debris. The ground is saturated with so much old oil, grease, and coal dust that it has become a kind of railroad asphalt. Over in one corner is a box of brand new brake pads for the big diesels, the last official residents of the old roundhouse. The turntable is still intact and functional but without traffic.

The locomotives may be gone but the old roundhouse is not entirely abandoned; a contingent of hobos and derelicts camp here every night, recent arrivals aboard the freight trains that pass through the yards. Their wine bottles and beer cans fill the pits. Trash is everywhere. Almost every window has been carefully broken by the people who visit the old roundhouse—broken human beings who seemingly want to share their condition with everything they touch. Anything that can be broken has been systematically destroyed, as if the ghosts of the old engines and the men and women who cared for them were an offense to these modern people who care for nothing.

The empty old engine house is full of ghosts of long-dead engines and engineers and the hordes of mechanics and laborers who groomed the iron horse. Stella "Susie" Torres was one of these. She died while we were writing this, at the respectable age of ninety-six; she worked here for a quarter of a century. Susie was already in her forties, a divorced mother of two, when she went to work in the roundhouse there during World War II, one of the army of women who took over railroad jobs from men inducted into the armed forces. Like a lot of other women at the time, she put on overalls and steel-toed boots and went to work at Southern Pacific's Lenzen roundhouse. Somebody started calling her "Susie," and the name stuck. So did the job; she enjoyed it so much that she stayed on after the war, helping with the transition from steam to diesel.

Susie Torres worked in the roundhouse until she retired in 1966. She worked as an oiler, an important task in the days of steam, and as a "wiper." She assisted with boiler maintenance during the days of steam, washing out the boilers, and she operated the turntable, right up till retirement at age 68.

Baldwin No. 28 on the turntable at the Sierra RR roundhouse at Jamestown, California, ready for a day's drayage.

Nevada Northern doesn't own a roundhouse, perhaps because its fleet of locomotives was never large enough to justify one. Instead, it uses a long engine house to shelter its most costly rolling stock. This Baldwin served the Nevada Northern from almost the beginning; when the line shut down, it was left in the engine house, protected from weather and vandals. Other than a rusty water tank in the tender and expired boiler certification, the engine was ready for service nine years later. Engine houses like this one, or roundhouses where more locomotives were serviced, once were found about 100 miles apart, all up and down America.

Roundhouses were sometimes built of brick and concrete, as fire resistant as possible. The pits between the tracks allowed oilers and mechanics to inspect and service the soft underbellies of the engines, but it was grimy work.

Corrugated iron was a quick, cheap building material for the little shortline operations to use on their roundhouses.

the Union Pacific as it went west from Lincoln, Nebraska. Local historian Tom Anderson recalls that there was at least one railroad family on every block in town. The shops buildings were some of the first major buildings built in Grand Island, and now only a few survive. A tornado did some damage years ago, but the railroad needed the shop, so it rebuilt immediately.

Roundhouses and the extensive shop complexes (and the hordes of shop workers) have gradually disappeared for one simple reason: they no longer are needed. The railroads discovered way back in the 1930s that diesel power was superior to steam in every way—except perhaps romantic and theatrical appeal. A steam locomotive needs to stop for fuel and water seven times more often than a diesel. When the first diesel freight locomotives were tested in 1938, they proved to be faster, more powerful, and required far less maintenance. It was obvious to everybody in the business that a quantum leap in railroad technology had been achieved.

Accountants don't factor romantic appeal or tradition into profit and loss statements; the steam

Top: Stella "Susie" Torres used to work this turntable in the Southern Pacific in San Jose, California, right up until she retired in 1976. No locomotives have used it for several years now; it and the roundhouse it served are both obsolete and considered a hazard.

Bottom left: Frank "Romey" Torres prepares to blow the steam whistle atop the Southern Pacific Lenzen Street roundhouse in San Jose, California, for the very last time, the day most of the building was torn down in 1956. The whistle itself was saved and is now in a private collection. Frank worked in the steam plant of the roundhouse; on his last day on the job before retirement, while training his replacement, he collapsed and died. *Mary Canchola collection*

Bottom right: Five of the women who worked in the Southern Pacific roundhouse in San Jose during World War II pose aboard one of the big steam locomotives used in passenger service on their division; Susie Torres is at the upper right. She adored working here and stayed on until mandatory retirement age. *Mary Canchola collection*

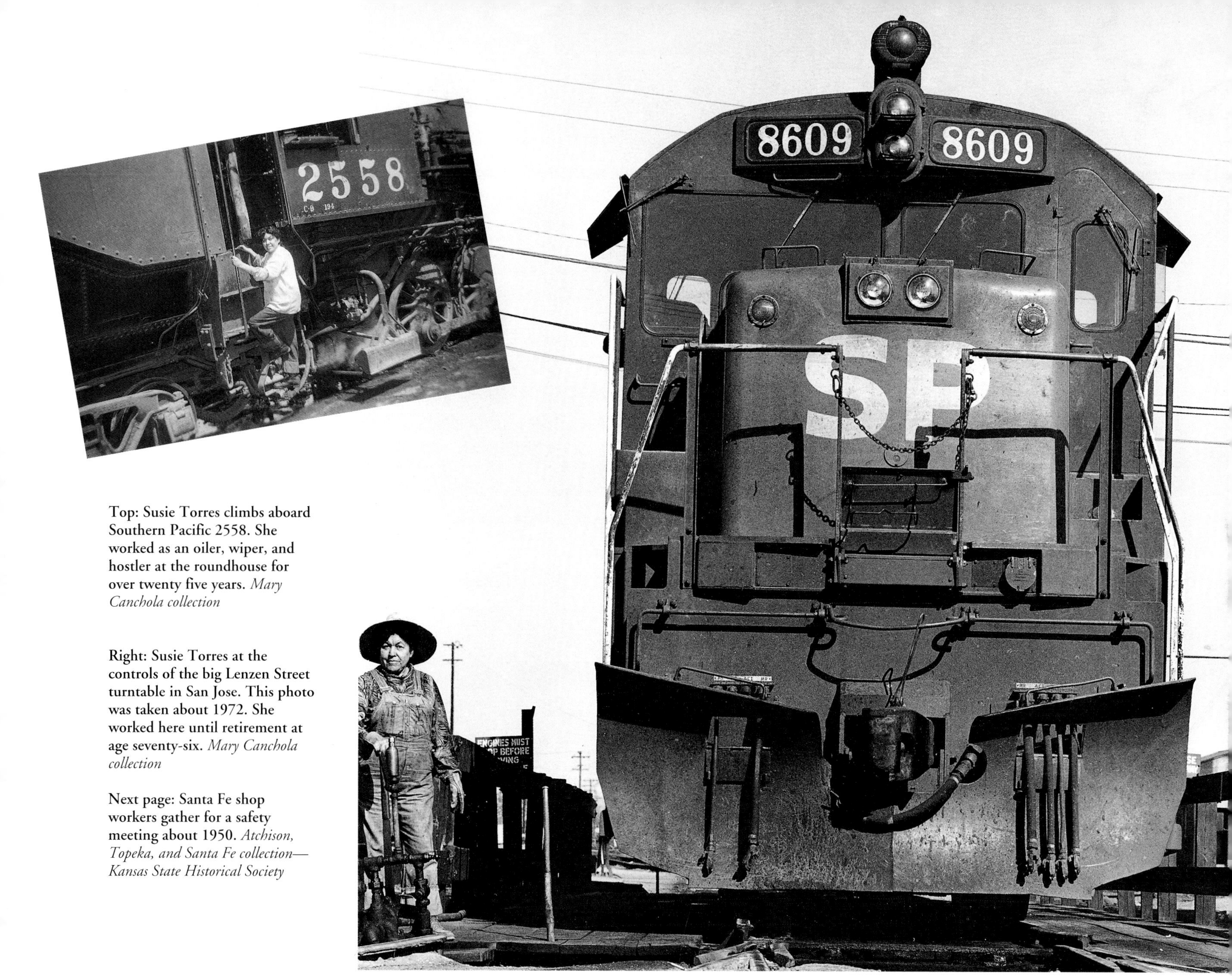

Top: Susie Torres climbs aboard Southern Pacific 2558. She worked as an oiler, wiper, and hostler at the roundhouse for over twenty five years. *Mary Canchola collection*

Right: Susie Torres at the controls of the big Lenzen Street turntable in San Jose. This photo was taken about 1972. She worked here until retirement at age seventy-six. *Mary Canchola collection*

Next page: Santa Fe shop workers gather for a safety meeting about 1950. *Atchison, Topeka, and Santa Fe collection—Kansas State Historical Society*

locomotives, the shops, and the people who serviced them quite suddenly became a luxury the industry could not afford. The locomotives were out of service by the mid-1950s. The men and women who made careers as boilermakers and pipefitters were scrapped shortly thereafter. The shops and roundhouses are still being torn down.

Top left: The rubble of the Georgia RR roundhouse at Atlanta, 1864. Confederate soldiers burned the place and abandoned the engines to this line just before the city was captured by Federal forces. Close inspection reveals that the loss might not have been such a long-term handicap, though; the building was designed for the very smallest of locomotives. *National Archives*

Top right: Replacing wheels on rolling stock was a common chore in roundhouses in the days of steam, and stacks of them piled up.

The Sierra Railroad Roundhouse, Jamestown, California

Although the little Sierra Railroad is just one of many obscure little short line relics of railroad history, you've seen it in action many times. In fact, just about everybody has seen this line's rolling stock in action because it has been used in hundreds of Hollywood motion pictures *(High Noon, My Little Chickadee, The Marx Brothers Go West, Back To The Future Part III)* and over 300 television programs.

Despite the association with Tinseltown, the little operation was—and still is—a transportation system that serves its community by carrying bulk cargo and freight... along with considerable numbers, these days, of rail fans. There is nothing phony or artificial about the rolling stock or the little roundhouse where the Sierra RR maintains its locomotives and cars.

The line was begun by Charles Crocker back in 1895, intended to link the forest product industry of the Sierra foothills with the Southern Pacific mainline at Oakley. The tracks reached the little old Gold Rush town of Jamestown two years later. A roundhouse was built here to serve the little line, and one of the first locomotives to roll into the place was Baldwin #3; it is still here, still pulling its weight after almost a hundred years in service.

Passenger service was discontinued in 1938, but the operation continues to operate as a freight carrier, and passengers are carried on tourist rides.

The roundhouse was built about 1897. A fire burned part of the structure about 1905, but the machine shop was undamaged and the structure was rebuilt around it as a four stall facility, and two other stalls were added in the 1920s. It has been in continuous operation now for nearly one hundred years.

Several women and a small child (foreground) pose in front of the roundhouse at Roswell, New Mexico, 1895. *Atchison, Topeka, and Santa Fe collection—Kansas State Historical Society*

The roundhouse gang at Topeka, Kansas, 1885. *Atchison, Topeka, and Santa Fe collection—Kansas State Historical Society*

Saving the Depots—A Short Course in Jams and Preserves

So... your town has a glorious little depot, unused for several years, and you hear the railroad wants to tear it down. It seems a real shame, you tell yourself, after all these years, to wreck something that could continue to be useful. After all, a lot of people in this community have experienced some of the most important moments of their life in that depot. And that building was built to last... you just can't get construction like that any more. It sure seems a shame that somebody can't do something! Is that somebody turning out to be... you?

Is a Depot Worth Saving?

Just ask a community who did it. If you have a sense that the well-being of your depot is somehow tied to the economic life of your town, you're right! A depot says a lot about its community. After all these years it continues to be an indicator of community values, wealth, and commitments. The presence of a real depot tells visitors they are welcome; it's an invitation to stop and chat, to sample the atmosphere of the town.

Maybe you live in a town whose local economy seems to be fading. And now the railroad wants to demolish the depot. Your town has a difficult time buying a new fire truck; how are they going to find the money to save a depot? How can you convince them that the depot is a critical component in the town's future? After all, the depot has been boarded up for years. Since it's hard to argue with success, let's look at a few towns where

Meet the sole surviving example of this depot type in Missouri, the Chicago & Alton RR depot at Independence, circa 1880. The railroad wants to tear it down or give it away, the local vandals want to deface it with graffiti, and a small community of preservation-minded folks in the community want very much to bring it back to its original glory. The latter seem to be winning, although it doesn't yet show. The preservation process begins with meetings, commitments, surveys, and research. Local architects, the state historic preservation program, the local chapter of the American Institute of Architects, and many local people are working hard to save this depot.

Top: One-hundred-and-fifteen years have taken their toll on the C&A depot, but the precision of its construction still shows through the peeling paint. The boards are still tight and the structure is still strong, according to the evaluation team. It's a good example of Eastlake style detailing; the decorations were cut out with jigsaws.

Bottom: This is the interior of Harry Truman's Independence, Missouri, depot in 1993 — scandalously neglected and vandalized, even though the depot is an active Amtrak stop. Before and after he was president of the United States, Truman liked to drop in here to chat and visit with the people who worked in this office. And his 1948 campaign started and ended at the Independence station. All depots created a little history, each in their own way; sadly, sometimes that history is endangered by abuse and neglect like this.

the depot, and the people who saved it, made a difference.

'One Thing Led to Another...' Santa Clara, California

The Santa Clara depot has the proud distinction of being the oldest operational depot in the West. It recently hosted an open house for 10,000 people, to celebrate the 130th anniversary of the opening of the historic San Francisco & San Jose Railroad. Why was the celebration held in Santa Clara rather than in adjacent, and much larger, San Jose? Because of the depot. Although the opening of the original rail line more than 130 years ago was held in San Jose, the original brick depot there had been demolished. Santa Clara's depot is the pride of the community and a joy to the daily commuters who use it.

The depot was restored by the South Bay Historical Railroad Society but as curator Ed Peterman recalls, "We didn't plan to restore a depot. We were just looking for some space for our model railroad club. It was one of those situations where one thing just led to another."

A common fate for many country depots is to serve as a freight building for a local feed store. This is a standard depot that once served Moreland, Kansas. On the bright side, the building is still standing and being maintained, which is better than being left to rot or torn down in favor of a parking lot.

At the time the Southern Pacific Railroad was still using the Santa Clara depot, but the attached freight room was being used by a trucking company. There was enough space for the model railroaders, but Southern Pacific wanted to negotiate with a chartered organization, not an informal club. The group quickly reorganized as a non-profit group, adding the word Historical to their name in order to satisfy charter requirements. It seemed a good idea at the time to include the functions of a museum and library, even though the only collections were privately owned by various club members.

The paperwork was filled out and sent in late 1985, and by January 1986 the club had a charter as a nonprofit historical society, and it had a building. But heavy use by the trucking company and deferred maintenance by Southern Pacific had left the place a wreck. The club faced a crisis. Most of

the original club members had joined to build model railroads, not chip paint all weekend. Fortunately there was a core group of dedicated individuals who saw the long-term benefits, and for the next several years the depot was restored and polished.

They applied for funding from all the usual sources, private, city, county, and federal. Eventually

Now here's an interesting preservation project: Grand Junction, Colorado's beefy old depot is one of the rare terminal buildings to use extensive tile and stone. It is, despite some peeling paint, in good shape and about to be restored to its original glory by a family with extensive local business activities, using their own money.

there was a new roof, new freight platform, and a completely restored depot and freight room. They matched the original paint and completely restored the exterior; then repainted when a more detailed analysis revealed the color had been several shades darker. Today the Santa Clara depot serves daily railroad commuters from the original ticket office. There is also a railroad library and research center in

The Grand Junction depot is going to stay right by the tracks, even though many depots have to be moved from the right-of-way to avoid destruction. The Leany family, which is financing and directing the restoration, isn't quite sure exactly what they're going to do with it, but it will be railroad-related.

the old depot. The adjacent freight room is large enough to hold three functions. One portion is devoted to a large museum and meeting room for local railroad societies. The second area is used by the model railroaders who have three layouts underway. And the old freight office at the far end is once again used for administrative offices, this time for the South Bay Historical Railroad Society.

Today the Santa Clara depot is the pride of the city of Santa Clara and attracts hundreds of rail fans and tourists. The community recently hosted an Open House in honor of the founding of the San Francisco & San Jose Railroad and 10,000 enthusiasts showed up to hear the politicians speak. Every weekend the depot is a meeting place for several dozen railroad enthusiasts and historians, some of them building models, some working on history projects, some organizing exhibits. This depot supports an extraordinary vitality in the community; this depot makes a difference.

Farmers' Market and Focal Point: Washington, Missouri

Front Street, along the Missouri River in the little town of Washington, was in desperate need of repair. Washington, just west of St. Louis, like many other river towns, had used the river front and the land near the rail lines for the town dump. The entire area along the railroad tracks needed attention. Environmental awareness was an important impetus

to this depot restoration project and plans for a major riverfront cleanup were underway.

Residents already knew their depot was important, probably the oldest one in the state. In 1855 the Pacific railroad completed 44 miles of track between Pacific, Missouri, and the river town of Hermann. At one time the Pacific railroad had aspired to be the first railroad to reach the Pacific Coast. The original passenger depot was lost in the Civil War, but the freight building, a block away, survived. By 1865 the freight building was serving as the town's depot. The town finally got a new passenger depot in 1923 and the old structure was again relegated to freight.

Fundraising and political hearings took several years but finally the joint efforts of the citizens, the Washington Historical Preservation Commission, the Chamber of Commerce, and the City of Washington all combined to preserve this depot. Original renovation plans considered using the depot as a Farmers' Market, a focal point for downtown activity in Washington. Today both the Pacific depot and the brick Missouri Pacific depot, built in 1923, are owned by the city. Painted to match the original yellow

This 1865 frame building is the Missouri Pacific depot at Washington, Missouri. The building has been preserved and left in place, alongside the tracks and adjacent to the Missouri River, which flows by in the background. A ceramics business occupied the building at the time this photo was shot in early 1994. Once again, while it's not a rail-related use of the building, it's good to see such a building being used and maintained.

and green, the old freight depot building also sports a new roof that took nearly two years to install. The Chamber of Commerce now operates the buildings, leasing them to arts-related groups.

Washington is a town that did some innovative negotiation with the railroad. A very active track borders the river although the trains no longer stop at this station. A portion of the Missouri Pacific right-of-way includes Front Street, which needed to be repaved. The railroad was reluctant to fund the cost of street repairs along Front Street, but they were willing to negotiate. So the railroad traded the two depots, but not the land, for the costs of repaving.

Volunteers from Washington Preservation, Inc., spent weekends painting and preserving the old depot, but the project was the joint effort of the Chamber of Commerce, the town of Washington, and the Washington Historical Preservation Commission. Commissioner Jo Ann Radetic recalls that the effort took several years from start to finish, beginning in 1987 and reopening in 1989. At first the city fathers were reluctant to commit money to the depot but finally consented. "The Washington city council grudgingly authorized additional city labor toward restoring the old frame freight depot building for a seasonal Farmer's Market," says the local paper in October 1987. Others were more confident and the fundraising efforts pressed on.

Was the renovation important to the vitality of the community? Absolutely. Although this town prefers a quiet life compared to neighboring St. Louis and the weekend river retreat town of Hermann, visitors en route to either town now stop and visit Washington. And Washington now has a unique and historic feature to share with the traveler who happens by. Today the riverfront is again scenic, the railroad has parted with two surplus eyesores, and the town of Washington has gained two revenue producing historic attractions.

Depot of Local History: Medicine Bow, Wyoming

It's hard to tell what fades first... does the town die because the depot is gone? Or did they close the depot because the town was fading? There are still a few wonderful little towns where it's pretty obvious that the depot remains as the heart of civic activity, even when passenger service is gone. Working together to save a depot has brought a new sense of community and economic vitality. It has literally saved the town.

Medicine Bow, Wyoming, could be called a one-horse town. You could even call it a one-horse,

The Trouble With Depots

There are a lot of depots! One publication by the National Trust puts the current number at 20,000, although that is half of the number of depots around during the 1950s. During the heyday of railroad construction, between about 1890 to 1925, competing railroads built depots to outshine the competition. Even small towns had three or four depots. Leavenworth, Kansas, for example, still has three remaining, including two passenger depots eligible for the National Register of Historic Places. In addition they have a little suburban depot just outside town in Lansing, Kansas. Which depot is the best... the most historic? Which one should the town try to save first? It is difficult for many communities to make an effort to save one depot, let alone three or four.

Answer: Leavenworth has saved all of their depots, and they all attract attention. The Union Station is now a community center, the Santa Fe depot is a Mexican restaurant, and the Burlington freight house is used by a business for storage. The Santa Fe depot at Lansing is going to be used as a museum. The new uses for these four depots are typical of the new uses of depots across the country.

Major metropolitan areas sometimes have a dozen or more depots worth saving. St. Louis, Missouri, has one of the grandest Union Stations in the world. It's a remarkable asset to the city and to the entire region. But the greater St. Louis area also has a dozen or so smaller depots, many of them also historic and still functioning as depots for rail traffic. The Florrisant depot is an office for the Chamber of Commerce, but the Kirkwood depot and the Eads Bridge still serve rail passengers. In the greater St. Louis area each depot has been carefully evaluated for a continued role in the transportation network.

And another dilemma presented by depots is their location. It would be a lot easier to find a new tenant for such a handsome building with adequate parking in the center of the downtown... if only it weren't located next to a noisy and dangerous railroad track! The larger depots and terminals, handsome brick or marble buildings, cannot be moved without incredible expense. And frequently the entire neighborhood around a railroad depot is in decay. It might be possible to save the depot, but resurrecting an entire neighborhood or business district is more than most preservation groups are willing to tackle.

However, one developer's location nightmare can be another developer's location dream. The depot in Palo Alto, California, has offered some surprising opportunities for housing development. Developers have built new housing within a very short walking distance of the depot to attract residents who ordinarily commute to San Francisco. So in some situations a very noisy and active railroad corridor is an asset rather than a liability.

two-building town. This is the West, the edge of the Continental Divide, the place where the antelope still play, every day. And Medicine Bow never heard the discouraging word when the railroad decided to discontinue passenger service.

Medicine Bow has two important buildings: its depot, built around 1905, and The Virginian Hotel, built a year or so later. Today travelers detour from Interstate 80 to drive through Medicine Bow just to get a sense of what frontier life had been like. This tiny town is the center for a much greater area in southeastern Wyoming . The depot is the museum, Chamber of Commerce, visitor center, and memorial garden for this ranching community. And the hotel is a great place to have a drink, to eat, and to sleep. Just leave your buggy right out front where travelers have tied up for ninety years.

It's a windy, wide open space. The Claghorn Ranch is nearby; it's been in the same family for more than a century. But the only lights shining at night in the deep Wyoming darkness are at the depot. It must have been a great comfort to prairie travelers to follow the lights of a train and find the warmth of a depot.

Many depots have been turned into a community museum, a place to preserve local history. In Medicine Bow the depot freight room now holds many of the personal collections that had once been stored in local spare rooms and sheds. But the

Previous page: Sometimes it's hard to tell that a renovated depot ever had any connection with the railroad industry, and that's what's happened to this old station. It's a mental health clinic now but it has been so extensively modified that virtually no clue to its original function remains except a big bay window and the set of tracks alongside one end of the building.

Here's another kind of preservation—this old depot at Millbrae, California, has been recycled as a railroad depot, a function it performs perfectly. The depot agent and his family don't live upstairs anymore but the place still opens for business at 5:30 a.m. every weekday, serving up tickets to passengers for the fifty passenger trains that stop here daily.

Tiny Florissant, Missouri, is a suburb of St. Louis and this little depot once served passengers on one of the local interurban trolley lines. It is a chamber of commerce office today, a pretty common use for old, obsolete depots—and a better alternative than a pile of rubble.

Medicine Bow depot already contained most of the local history for the area. It was already the center of community vitality, so it didn't have to change much. Today it is the Genuine Article, a depot that still gives you the feel that the station agent just stepped over to the hotel to take them their mail. Medicine Bow may be one of the very few depot museums that retains the flavor of how the station agent really lived in the depot.

In communities where housing was not available, the station agent and family lived at the depot. Typical depots had family living quarters on one end and the freight room on the other. The agent's office in the middle of the depot had a telegrapher's key, train orders, and all the required railroad records. The adjacent waiting room served the occasional passenger. Even though Medicine Bow was on a trunk line, passengers seldom passed through this little depot, but each one that arrived became something of a special event. So smaller depots like Medicine Bow were always a focal point in their community, a regular link with the wide wonderful world far away. And they offered a chance to catch up on all the local news as soon as you arrived.

Today Medicine Bow has a chain-link fence between the tracks and the depot. But not too much else has changed. The quilts and antimacassars, the tea kettle and the mending, all part of the life of a railroad agent's family on the frontier are still evident in Medicine Bow. You can still drop in to the depot anytime to catch up on the news. This depot still makes the difference.

A Quick Look Back at Preservation Efforts

The preservation and restoration of a railroad depot, or any other public building for that matter, is a fairly new phenomena. Over the years a few public monuments have been saved, mostly due to the extraordinary efforts of a few private individuals. It is hard to believe that even Mount Vernon was once slated for a subdivision. And the creation of the wonderful National Historic Site at Promontory, Utah, was the due to the efforts of a single individual, Bernice Gibbs Anderson. She lobbied for nearly forty years to set aside the site at Promontory in order to properly celebrate the centennial anniversary of the Golden Spike ceremony in 1969. Her goal was realized in 1965, leaving just a few years to prepare for a suitable ceremony.

Railroad depot preservation has especially escalated in the last two decades. This is due in great part to the abandonment of depots by the railroads as service was consolidated and shifted. Depots were becoming available because the railroads no longer needed them. But it is also due to a fundamental shift in public attitude. The demolition of the Pennsylvania Station in 1963 had a profound effect on many citizens. The federal National Historic Preservation Act of 1966 and the creation of many local and state preservation ordinances were a direct result of that dark day in 1963.

In addition, the railroads themselves have changed their attitudes. Railroads realize that railroad enthusiasts, retirees, preservationists... the rail fans, are important to our nation's railroads. Those hundreds of people who are interested in the American rail system are the very people who write letters to Congress when railroads need support. So several of the major railroads now have museums with pro-

fessional archival staff devoted to the history of their particular company. Preserving a local depot helps maintain community awareness of the railroad industry.

So there is a different attitude about demolition these days. It's due in part to an awareness of environmental issues. People are more aware that some resources are limited. It's also due to an optimism that other alternatives might be available. And it's due to a willingness to work together, railroads, community, and preservationists. Depots, however, come with a few built-in problems that

The people of Atchison, Kansas, turned their big old depot into a museum celebrating the town's association with Santa Fe, another common application for old depots.

The Kansas City Terminal Railroad Association owns many of the tracks that run through the middle of Kansas City, and they built the terminal, too.

make re-use difficult. Let's look at a few of the problems.

Saving a Depot... Where Do You Start?

In the beginning it will seem that you have to make all sorts of decisions all at the same time. You have to make sure the structure is safe at the same time you are negotiating its future. You have to do fundraising at the same time you are meeting with railroad representatives. How do you decide what to do first?

Before you start...STOP! Resist the temptation to bring in the dumpster and the paint crew. Do not clean the graffiti or tidy up the train yard. And do not allow well-meaning railroad memorabilia scavengers to remove that old pile of scrap rail, discarded ties, wig-wags, signal boxes, and crossing arms, even if you happen to be related to a salvage enthusiast. Do not scrape paint or replace windows. You need to make two calls. Call your State Historic Preservation Office and call the National Trust for Historic Preservation before you proceed.

While it may look like rubbish, important artifacts can be found laying around the depot site. The location of these discards can be important to reconstructing this depot's past. And some of the most fascinating history is frequently found on the walls inside the freight room. Freight agents frequently noted their initials and the years of their service on the wall. So enlist the aid of an expert...call your State Historic Preservation Office.

Depot preservation has become a little easier since there are now dozens of projects that add up to years of experience... we have learned a few things from the efforts of others. Your regional National Trust office will probably tell you about the Depot Database, coordinated in the Denver office of the National Trust for Historic Preservation. And they will make arrangements to send you an important sixteen-page booklet, "Railroad Depot Acquisition and Development." But until the doctor arrives, here are some very general guidelines.

First and foremost, make the building safe. Be sure it's locked up, boarded up, and has a roof on it. Keep vandals and varmints out. If it is still railroad property, the railroad may give you some help on this. Keeping the weather and transients out preserves the structure in the short term. If possible, put a sign on the building so that passersby know there is a preservation effort underway. Rail fans and tourists are attracted to depots and will help spread the word if a sign is on or near the depot. And a sign prevents vandalism. Many people help themselves to

Kansas City's Union Station has been preserved in a state of slightly arrested decay, a massive Beaux-Arts building beloved by many in the community. The problem for Kansas City, now that legal obstacles to renovation of the old Union Station have been removed, is—just what do you do with a beautiful old building that costs a quarter of a million dollars a year to heat and cool? How do you make it pay its own keep?

parts of a building because they presume... "it will just be torn down anyway. Might as well get a souvenir while I can." So it reminds collectors that this building has a future.

Second, talk to every group you can. Even if you don't have a plan yet, start letting politicians know that people are thinking about saving this building. Talk to the Chamber of Commerce, the town Council, the elected officials from your state, anyone and everyone. Talk to the Scouts, the Lodge, and the Historic Museums. You don't have to have a new use for the building at this point, but it is really important to have a wide base of interest and support. And you'll be surprised how many clubs and organizations will help you with fundraising later on.

Since you have already contacted your State Historic Preservation Office, they have suggested how to have your depot evaluated. And you will have acquired a booklet from the National Trust which outlines the usual steps in the depot preservation process. While you are going to meetings and talking to people, get a professional architect, engineer, or contractor to assess the building's physical condition.

The National Trust booklet "Railroad Depot Acquisition and Development" outlines eight common steps in the depot preservation process. It starts with Step One, a structural evaluation of the building, and proceeds through the process of negotiation with the railroad. The booklet walks you through the process of defining your project, securing public support, and preparing your documentation. But there are a few things that usually happen before Step One and a few more after Step Eight.

Before Step One, "Building Evaluation," you will already have talked with a lot of people. Talking to everyone in town accomplishes several things. While you are educating the public about your depot project, you will also be gathering important feedback from the community concerning the best use for the depot. And you will get a sense of the type of community support available for such a project. This is a two-way process. While you are talking about the depot you are also shaping public opinion. So give people some time and some room to change their minds about saving the depot, especially if they seem a little skeptical at first. Talk to

Friends of the El Dorado, Kansas, depot are trying to raise enough money , to bring the handsome station back to some sort of life, but it takes a lot of money and the community is small—a common problem for communities all over the United States and Canada.

everybody. And it will probably pay to go back again when the project is underway, to bring your community up-to-date on progress.

Even if your town or local government is not willing to take on a depot preservation project themselves, their support is key to the success of the project. Railroad companies are more willing to negotiate with local officials, in the belief that governments are more permanent than a local group of volunteers or enthusiasts. And you may find that a government group actually has some negotiating leverage with the railroad.

People who have preserved and restored depots say that negotiating with the railroad was actually one of the easier parts of the whole process. The hardest part, the most time-consuming and the most frustrating, were the dozens of meetings and public hearings. Marriages and friendships can be strained by the seemingly endless discussions about a vacant depot. So all of those phone calls and meetings and discussions, all of those cookies and cups of coffee, are a time-consuming but essential part of your lobbying efforts.

After Step Eight, "Submit the final plan to the railroad company," the real fun begins. When the depot finally belongs to you, then the restoration work can begin. And after the restoration and the grand reopening, your depot will need an occupant. Since your

Fairbury, Nebraska, is restoring its big depot slowly, with volunteers, and is making some headway. It's a unique project, a salute to the Rock Island railroaders who used to call Fairbury home. Fairbury used to house railroad administration offices as well as passengers in this depot. The freight buildings, roundhouse, and shops were located nearby.

Abilene, Texas, is in the process of cleaning up this nice station; asbestos tile was being removed when this photograph was made.

depot is probably not going to be in the railroad business anymore, you will need to find a suitable occupant for the structure. This is when all of the talking and meeting that you did at the beginning will finally pay off. Most of the time a good use for the building evolves from the meetings and discussions. So the more people that become involved with the depot, the more options you are likely to have when a new tenant needs to be found.

Is My Depot Historic... and What Does that Mean?

Since most of the railroad buildings in America were built before World War II they meet the first test of a historic artifact... age. It has to be at least 50 years old to officially be considered historic. (Yes, there is a loophole. But your building has to be absolutely extraordinary to be nominated if it is less than 50 years old.)

If your depot is an important and historic depot, it might be eligible for special funding that would help in its restoration. Many depots, roundhouses, and other railroad structures already appear on an inventory of historic resources, listed with your State Office of Historic Preservation. All old buildings have a past... and a history. But not all old buildings are officially historic. So to determine if your depot meets the official criteria, someone will have to do a little research on the depot.

The first place to start is with your local Historical Society or Historic Landmarks Commission. Find out if someone else has already done the research. Contact the State Office of Historic Preservation to determine if your depot already appears on

Depot and Railroad Preservation Organizations

The Railroad Station Historical Society

The Society was founded in 1968 and is still an all-volunteer organization. It is a small group that is constantly maintaining an inventory of railroad structures. They publish a newsletter six times a year and at least one extended monograph on a railroad subject. Address inquiries to: The Railroad Station Historical Society, 430 Ivy Ave., Crete, Nebraska 68333.

The National Railway Historical Society (NRHS)

This is probably the largest and most active railroad history group. With 150 chapters it undertakes a wide variety of activities for preservationists, rail fans and railroad retirees. They can be contacted at: National Railway Historical Society, 1-A Rich Court, Ho-Ho-Kus, NJ 07423.

Railway and Locomotive Historical Society

This is still another important resource. This group focuses on information helpful to serious railroad property preservation. It is a good resource for technical information. Contact: The Railway and Locomotive Historical Society, c/o H. Arnold Wilder, 46 Lowell Road, Westford, Mass. 01886

The National Association of Railroad Passengers (NARP)

NARP is dedicated to keeping depots available to serve travelers... and commuters. Travel by train and rail transit is no longer an option in many areas, even though the railroad tracks are still there, and the train thunders by on a regular schedule. In many cases existing depots are underutilized or ignored. Sometimes passengers are served with an "Amshack" shelter, occasionally located on the platform of the old depot. NARP seeks better service for the rail passenger.

NARP has a book highlighting 400 depots all across the nation, historic and interesting depots that still remain along the Amtrak routes. These depots have been identified by NARP as being eligible for funds under the ISTEA program, a federal program that provides construction money. Membership, donations, and book information are available from:

National Association of Railroad Passengers, 900 Second Street, N.E., Suite 308, Washington, D. C., 20002-3557.

their inventory list. Many state offices have completed an inventory of all the known depot buildings that are over fifty years old. And some already have some preliminary research work completed. But this is just a list of structures that meets the first criteria of age. Just because your depot appears on an inventory does not mean it is historic, just old. What if it's not on the inventory? If you find your depot or railroad structure is over fifty years old and has somehow been omitted from the basic inventory list... wave the red flag! All good railroaders know how to get attention when it's important!

Who Decides if a Depot is Officially Historic?

Again, it is the State Historic Preservation Office, a state agency that makes the evaluation, based on research information sent to them by the local community. The application forms are available from the SHPO. The application and all of the research material goes to an independent panel of historians and architects. They review the application and make a recommendation to the State. If the building meets the criteria to be considered historic,

The MoPac depot is still in fine shape here in "Jeff City," Missouri, but the only folks allowed inside work for the railroad; it is used for offices now, another way depots manage to survive.

The beautiful depot at Evanston, Wyoming, has been restored and is used by Amtrak. It's an important part of Evanston, which has historically been a railroad town. In the nineteenth century, maintenance and repair shops of the Central Pacific railroad were located here. While the depot is beautiful, it is not a historic building by itself. However, it is an important part of the city's downtown and contributes to the character of the downtown area, which is a National Historic District.

it is placed on the State Register. And once a building is designated historic by the state, it is then considered to be eligible to be included on the National Register; there is not a second evaluation process at this time.

Whether you're collecting baseball cards, dolls, or antique furniture, there are some basic yardsticks to determine value and importance. And the same holds true for railroad depots. Age and scarcity are important considerations. So are design, workmanship, and methods of construction. The standards applied by the state and used for the National Register were developed by the Department of the Interior. Many states and counties have also adopted these standards and forms for local historic evaluations. So all depots across the country are evaluated by the same set of standards, without local favoritism or bias.

What Makes a Railroad Building Historic?

There are four criteria for historic significance; your depot must be shown to be significant in at least one of these four. And not only does your depot have to meet a level of significance within its criteria, it also has to be judged significant within its historic context.

For example, the historic context for railroad depots is almost always railroad history. Although you might possibly compare the architectural merit of depots with the architecture of other public buildings, the most reasonable historic context for depots is railroad development. Now let's look a little more closely at the four criteria.

The first criteria is for buildings that are associated with an important event in American history. Your depot might be associated with an event that made a "significant contribution to the broad pattern of our history." The "Truman" depot in Independence, Missouri, is a depot with national historic significance. It's not because it is the depot in Harry Truman's hometown, and not because Harry and Bess preferred rail travel. The Independence depot is important because of the role of this depot and the railroad in Truman's 1948 campaign strategy.

Truman had been told he was the underdog in the election. He decided to take his presidential campaign to the voters, and he determined that the best way to reach the average voter in America at that time was to travel by train. The whistle-stop campaign reached thousands of citizens who still did not have an automobile and had no other way to see a candidate. Harry Truman spoke from the back platform of the last car on the train. It was a campaign that started and ended at the Independence station, a campaign that won an election and changed American history. Its important role in American history qualifies the Independence depot for national significance.

A second criteria includes buildings that are associated with the lives of persons significant to our past. The property is usually associated with the person during the productive period of his life, reflecting the period in which they achieved prominence. The family home of railroad builder James J. Hill is an extraordinary mansion on the hill overlooking downtown St. Paul, Minnesota. The thirty-six room mansion was built for James and Mary Hill, their nine children, and twelve live-in servants. Although it is an impressive mansion by any standard, it qualifies for the National Register because of its association with railroad builder James J. Hill.

But dozens of promoters and capitalists built railroads, why is James J. Hill special? Because Hill built the Great Northern Railroad between St. Paul and Seattle in 1883, without the government subsidies that had supported the construction of other railroad lines. The Hill railroads were probably the single most im-

portant element in the opening of the upper portion of America to settlement and development. So James J. Hill's role in the development of the West qualify his home as historic under the second criteria.

A third criteria includes buildings that "embody distinctive characteristics of a type, period, or method of construction..." This also includes depots that represent the work or a master, or possess high artistic value. This category covers a wide range of depots, roundhouses, and shops. For example, if a depot is the last one of its type in existence, even if it looks run-down and insignificant in appearance, it qualifies as historic under this classification. The depot at Marthasville, Missouri, fits into this category because it is so rare; it possesses the "distinct characteristics of a type."

This category also has a special provision that covers "ordinary depots." If the building is one com-

The people of Evanston, Wyoming, restored their 1900 depot to virtually new condition, inside and out, and it's now one of the nicest buildings in the whole town. Restored depots like this can and frequently are community focal points and draws for tourism, and that's what's happened for this town.

ponent in a group of buildings that are important, and the whole area qualifies as a historic district, then the depot itself is considered historic because it is included in the district. For example, the jewel of a depot at Evanston, Wyoming, a delightfully restored structure used by Amtrak, qualifies as an important part of the historic railroad town of Evanston. This town in the western Wyoming was an important focus for railroad activity in the nineteenth century, when the maintenance and repair shops for the Central Pacific railroad were located here. The downtown which includes the depot, is a National Historic District. Although the depot is beautiful, it is not a historic building by itself. However, it is an important structure in the downtown and contributes to the character of the Historic District.

Craftsmanship and design are important considerations included under the third criteria. We are aware that art and craftsmanship are expensive. As a society we may never again be able to afford the luxury of the wonderful sculptural detailings found in some of our depots. Bas-relief features of local flora and fauna, the local history depicted in the WPA murals inside the depots, the craftsmanship of the fireplaces in the waiting rooms... all these details speak volumes about the talents of the designer and local craftsmen as well as the values of the surrounding community.

We now realize that the Golden Age of railroad building took place when architects were developing an "American style." No longer satisfied with imitating Greek temples, Roman baths, or Gothic cathedrals, architects such as Bostonian Henry Hobson Richardson explored new design expressions for public buildings including depots. Widely imitated, Richardsonian-style depots appear in such places as Sedalia, Missouri, and Cheyenne, Wyoming. So we recognize many of our railroad depots as significant architectural treasures, demonstrating the finest design available, and we make every effort to preserve this heritage.

The last criteria includes structures that have yielded, or may yet yield, information important to our history. The sites of the roundhouse in Oneonta, New York, and the shops and roundhouse at Fairbury, Nebraska, are examples of sites that could qualify as historic under the fourth criteria. So even if the oldest buildings in an old railroad complex have been razed by a landlord that hopes to sell the property for development, even if all that remains of the roundhouse is the pit, it may still be worthwhile to preserve the site for future study.

What are the Benefits of Historic Registration?

Benefits fall into three areas. First, the property becomes eligible for money, usually federal or state preservation grants and federal tax credits. Second, the property is recognized as significant to the community, state, or nation. And last, the property frequently attracts a level of attention and appreciation that is an indirect economic benefit to the community.

Properties that have been documented and evaluated are listed annually in the National Register of Historic Places. These sites attract attention and visitor interest—and those visitors and tourists spend money while visiting the community. Loss of a National Historic District can mean the loss of an important economic asset in a community. When downtown Santa Cruz, California, was destroyed by an earthquake in 1989, many of its quake-damaged historic buildings were later bulldozed. Downtown Santa Cruz no longer has a National Register district; its unique character has been replaced by contemporary structures.

A registered site can frequently be an important educational resource to the local school district and to the larger community. Many National Register sites offer special tours, workshops, films, and classes for schools who are interested in using the site to teach students about their heritage. And a site that appears on the National Register of Historic Places gives the town a unique identity. Thousands of visitors travel to East Ely, Nevada, to see the Nevada Northern Railroad; it is an important destination even though there are no other "attractions" for hundreds of miles.

Does My Depot Have to be Historic to Be Saved?

What if my town's depot is a plain vanilla building that the railroad doesn't want any more? Does it have to be historic to be saved? The answer, of course, is that it does not have to be a landmark to be worth saving. Many extraordinary collections of all kinds are the work of individuals who have preserved railroad artifacts for personal satisfaction. And that includes steam locomotives, cabooses, roundhouses, and depots. Many an individual has acquired a depot for use as a home, a business building, or a storage shed. In some cases the depot has been moved; in others the depot stayed on site and a safety barricade was built between the depot and the tracks. Let's look at some examples of depots that have been recycled. Some have found new life in the railroad business; some have been recycled for "adaptive reuse."

Here's a hardworking depot in the middle of town. This rugged brick structure in Brigham City, Utah, is used as an office and locker room for the railroad crews. Passengers drive to nearby Ogden to board the Amtrak, but this building earns its keep with a different assignment.

Railroad Depots as a Tourist Attraction: Focal Points in the Local Economy

There is a resurgence of interest in passenger excursion lines, which can serve as a rolling setting for romantic dinners on short trips. Historic engines and passenger lines are being rediscovered by a new variety of rail-fan, the "heritage traveler." This individual seeks out adventures on a rail line just for the pleasure and unique experience of rail travel. So many of these little lines have been rediscovered in the last twenty years, that there are now several consultants who specialize in railroad tour development. They offer services to communities and individuals who want to develop marketing plans and cost analyses for surplus rail lines and depots.

And... Other Uses for Old Depots

The best use for any building is the use for which it was designed. Railroad buildings work best as railroad buildings. But sometimes it's just not practical... what then? Depots have been relocated and recycled into many other uses; let's look at some a samples.

Looking at a 1989 inventory of about 180 depots on one major railroad line in California, we see twelve depots are still in use with part of a depot function, a

Like the Brigham City, Utah, depot, this depot in Perry, Oklahoma, serves as an office and general use facility for the railroad maintenance crews.

crew office, or a freight office. Another thirteen are used by the railroad for a function that used to be housed in another type of railroad structure... maintenance offices for example. And twenty-nine were sold to a commuter line, along with the right-of-way and rolling stock, to use for interurban traffic.

Over one hundred depots have been moved. Twenty were moved to one park or another to serve as a local history museum or a transportation museum. About ten are now private residences. The remaining seventy or so now serve some private business or community function. A few belong to the local Chamber of Commerce. Many house a business that make use of the freight warehouse for bulk storage. Feed and grain stores, roofing companies, or flooring installers are pretty typical re-users for depots. Of the remaining structures, three had been demolished, three were being leased to Amtrak, and the remaining ones were boarded up, waiting for the next step.

Selecting a Good Use: Grand Island, Nebraska

What is the best use for an old railroad depot, an old locomotive shop, or an old roundhouse? How about using it as a depot, shop, or roundhouse? A surprising number of old railroad facilities are being sold to new shortline railroads. With the current trend toward large contracts and long-haul business, many feeder lines are being abandoned or sold to short-line operators. Short-line railroads, hauling seasonal ton-

The Roundhouse in Huron, South Dakota

A working roundhouse with full stalls is an extremely rare sight. Strange to believe, this may be one of the last real working roundhouses in America. It was saved by a regional railroad, the Dakota, Minnesota, and Eastern (DM&E), which is reusing facilities from an earlier time and an earlier railroad. Operating on a shoestring, this carrier is putting all its capital into equipment, not buildings. So the DM&E was lucky to find this old roundhouse to use for its operations. This roundhouse is even more rare because it is a surviving building from the old Chicago & North Western Railroad. This old rail line demolished most of its structures as soon as they were surplus. Made of buff-colored chacca brick, it is a rare sight and a rare building.

nage such as the corn harvest, have found ways to wring profitability out of a local line. Nebraska Central is a new shortline, and it has taken over the century old shop building in Grand Island, Nebraska. This is a remarkable building. Unlike most shops, this one is so clean you can eat off the floor.

Grand Island used to be a big railroad town. Historian Tom Anderson remembers that there used to be a railroad family living in nearly every block. When the Union Pacific was driving west to complete the transcontinental railroad, the first big shops and roundhouses west of Lincoln, Nebraska, were located in Grand Island. This shop building dates from that era, although it had to be substantially rebuilt when a tornado came through town. This particular building was probably first used as a machine shop for the steam locomotives, but it is still the right size for the diesels it services now.

Renovation, Rehabilitation and Restoration: Doing it Right

There are varying degrees of preservation... and related expense. Saving a depot does not automatically mean that it has to be restored to mint condition. In fact many individuals who enthusiastically "restore" an old structure inadvertently remove original material in order to replace it with a reproduction that is "prettier" or cleaner. If a building is historic and eligible for the National Register, certain restoration criteria apply. These are the standards for restoration set forth in the Department of the Interior guidelines.

But many depots would have been lost long ago if they all had to meet these exacting standards. Fortunately, there is more than one way to save a depot. And many, many depot buildings have been lovingly and inexpensively preserved by the personal efforts of ordinary folks with limited budgets. What are the differences in the varying levels? One contractor put it this way: "renovation means paint it, rehabilitation means paint it and put a new roof on it. Restoration means paint it, replace the roof with something that looks like the original, and install an old toilet."

And finally, a word of caution. While not every depot needs to be completely restored to be enjoyed, depot owners should be sensitive to the limitations of the structure. Not every depot can be modified to comfortably accommodate a restaurant or a museum. Making extreme alterations to the interior can limit the use of the building for subsequent owners. So it pays to look around and learn from the experiences and the mistakes of others.

Preservation Resources: How to Get Started

We suggest a phone call to either your regional National Trust Office or your State Historic Preservation Office. They will send lists of resources, suggest books to read, and people to talk to. They can give you an idea of the size of your task and provide moral support! Even if your depot or railroad building is not and will never be a registered landmark, these organizations will help. Your taxes support both of these institutions; they are interested in your project.

National Trust for Historic Preservation

The National Trust was chartered by Congress in 1949 to further our national policy of preserving our heritage. One of the primary jobs of the National Trust is to help citizens who want to save a building. To help depot preservationists, the National Trust also maintains a nationwide depot database through its Denver Office. This database currently includes information on about 650 depot preservation projects that have already been started. The major purpose of the database is to link new depot projects with successful and completed projects. So if you call them they will match your town with depot projects of similar size.

The National Trust also has a very helpful 16-page booklet "Railroad Depot Acquisition and Development," written in 1991, which offers a good

Strasburg, Colorado. This is a "standard structure" but it shore is purty. You can identify this gleaming building as a depot immediately, even though it has been moved away from the tracks. It serves its community as a county museum, an important focal structure in a cluster of preserved buildings. Its companion structures from frontier Colorado, also relocated to the museum grounds, include a one-room schoolhouse, a homesteaders' cabin, a windmill, a telephone booth, and an outhouse.

outline of how to proceed. Your Trust office can send you a copy. (Contact information for regional outlets is listed in the appendices.)

State Historic Preservation Office (SHPO)

Usually located in your state capital, the Historical Preservation Office is another important resource. Every state is required by federal statute to have such an office. The staff of your SHPO is probably already aware of the condition of your depot. Most states have a comprehensive inventory of historic sites, including depots and other railroad structures. The SHPO staff will be very glad that someone like you is taking a personal interest in this depot.

Both the National Trust and the SHPO can suggest places to look for restoration money. There are a number of federal and state funding programs that are available, and they do keep an eye on current funding legislation. They also can help with local resources. Working hand-in-hand with the National Trust, your state preservation office may already have extensive information about historic railroads and depots in your state. Their offices are usually in the state capital; some large state also have regional field offices.

State, County and City Historical Societies

An important resource for information and photographs of your depot and your town is usually your State Historical Society. The photographic archives of these sources are amazing. Some state historical societies were founded before the state itself

was admitted to the Union. And some have photographic collections that contain more than 100,000 images, usually including a depot or two.

And don't overlook the expertise and experience of your County or City Historical Society, if you are fortunate enough to have one. Sometimes they also maintain an archive and are happy to assist with research. Most counties also have a Landmarks Commission or a Historical Review Committee. They can be a tremendous help to you in your depot preservation effort.

The depot at Marthasville, Missouri, is considered to "embody distinctive characteristics of a type, period, or method of construction..." so it was a suitable candidate for restoration and preservation. If a depot is the last one of its type in existence, even if it looks run-down and insignificant in appearance, it qualifies as historic under this classification. Simple but well made, the Marthasville depot stands strong today.

Appendices

Places to Visit

Nearly every state commemorates its own railroad history with a railroad museum or railroad history collection. But several states house their railroad memorabilia in restored, working depots. The most outstanding examples are:

Utah State Railroad Museum, Ogden Union Station, Ogden, UT 84401

Railtown 1897 State Historic Park, End of 5th Avenue, P.O. Box 1250, Jamestown, CA 95327, 209/984-3953

Nevada Northern Railroad Museum, P.O. Box 150040, East Ely, NV 89315-0040, 702/289-2085

Baltimore and Ohio Railroad Museum, 901 W. Pratt, Baltimore, MD 21223, 410/752-2490

California State Railroad Museum, 111 "I" St., Old Sacramento, CA 95814, 916/552-5252, ext. 7245

Colorado Railroad Museum, 17155 W. 44th Ave., Golden, CO 80402, 303/279-4591

Golden Gate Railroad Museum, P.O. Box 3315, Redwood City, CA 94064, 415/363-2472

Magazines & Periodicals

We found various magazines to be helpful and inspirational. If you are fortunate enough to have a hobby shop that serves model railroaders, many magazines and books will probably be available there. Our favorites are:

Locomotive & Railway Preservation.

The magazine for the Preservation and Operation of Historic Railroad Equipment, published bimonthly by the Interurban Press, P.O. Box 379, Waukesha, WI 53817.

TRAINS The Magazine of Railroading

The publishers underlined "The" in their title so we will, too. It's a current newsmagazine for the railroad industry. Kalmbach Publishing Co., 21027 Crossroads Circle, P.O. Box 1612 Waukesha, WI 53187

Offices of the National Trust for Historic Preservation

Founded by Congress in 1949, the National Trust was created to preserve our national heritage. They advise and support citizens who undertake preservation projects. Currently they work from a national office in Washington, D. C. and seven regional offices.

National Trust for Historic Preservation National Headquarters
1785 Massachusetts Ave. N.W.
Washington, D.C. 20036
202/673-4296

Northeast Regional Office
7 Faneuil Hall Marketplace, 5th floor
Boston, MA 02109
617/523-0885
Serving: Connecticut, Maine, Massachusetts, New Hampshire, New York, Rhode Island, Vermont

Mid-Atlantic Regional Office
6401 Germantown Ave.
Philadelphia, PA 19144
215/438-2886
Serving: Delaware, District of Columbia, Maryland, New Jersey, Pennsylvania, Puerto Rico, Virgin Islands, Virginia, West Virginia

Southern Regional Office
456 King St.
Charleston, SC 29403
803/722-8552
Serving: Alabama, Arkansas, Florida, Georgia, Kentucky, Louisiana, Mississippi, North Carolina, South Carolina, Tennessee

Midwest Regional Office
53 W. Jackson Blvd., Suite 1135
Chicago, IL 60604
312/939-5547
Serving: Illinois, Indiana, Iowa, Michigan, Minnesota, Missouri, Ohio, Wisconsin

Mountain/Plains Regional Office
910 16th St., Suite 1100
Denver, CO 80202
303/623-1504
Serving: Colorado, Kansas, Montana, Nebraska, North Dakota, South Dakota, Oklahoma, Wyoming
Note: Call the Denver Office to contact the DEPOT DATABASE

Texas/New Mexico Field Office
500 Main Street, Suite 606
Fort Worth, TX 76102
817/332-4398
Serving: Texas, New Mexico

Western Regional Office
One Sutter St., Suite 707
San Francisco, CA 94104
415/956-0610
Serving: Alaska, Arizona, California, Guam, Hawaii, Idaho, Micronesia, Nevada, Oregon, Utah, Washington

Bibliography

We relied on the research efforts of scores of others; all of them know a lot more about depots than we know.

The American Railway, Its Construction, Development, Management, and Appliances. Bramhall House, New York, 1888. Reprinted 1970.

The Country Railroad Station in America. H. Roger Grant and Charles W. Bohi. The Center for Western Studies, Augustana College, Sioux Falls, South Dakota. 1988.

The History of the New York Central System. Aaron E. Klein, Bonanza Books, Crown Publishers Inc., 1985.

Kansas City and the Railroads. Charles N. Glaab, University Press of Kansas, Lawrence, Kansas 1993

Mary Colter: Builder Upon the Red Earth. Virginia L. Grattan, Northland Press, Flagstaff, Arizona. 1980

Meals by Fred Harvey. James David Henderson, Omni Publications, Hawthorne, California. Revised 1985.

North American Railroad Stations. Julian Cavalier, A.S. Barnes and Company, Inc. Cranbury, NJ 08512 (1977).

Photographing the Frontier. Dorothy and Thomas Hoobler, G. P. Putnam's Sons, New York, 1980.

Prune Country Railroading: Steel Trails to San Jose Norman W. Holmes, Shade Tree Books, Huntington Beach, CA 92647, 1985

Railroad Stations of New England Today, Volume 1. Mark W. Beauregard, Railroad Avenue Enterprises, Inc., Flanders, New Jersey 07836.

Railway Architecture. Written by members and associates of SAVE Britain's Heritage; edited by Marcus Binney and David Pearce. Van Norstrand Reinhold Company, New York 1979.

Railways: Past Present & Future. G. Freeman Allen, William Morrow and Company, Inc., New York, 1982

Train Shed Cyclopedia, Buildings and Structures of the American Railroads, 1893. Newton K. Gregg/Publisher, Novato, CA December 1975. This is a wonderful series of softcover books that contain reprints of selected chapters from an 1893 Railroad Reference Book. The original was written as a handbook for railroad managers and master mechanics. Originally published as a textbook by John Wiley & Sons, New York in 1893.

Waiting for the 5:05. Terminal, Station and Depot in America. Clay Lancaster, compiled by Lawrence Grow. Main Street/Universe Books, New York 1977. This book was published to accompany an exhibition of photographs and architectural drawings of depots from the Smithsonian.

"The History of the San Francisco and San Jose Railroad," Louis Richard Miller. Master's Thesis, 1947 (MA-History) University of California, Berkeley.

The Julian Cavalier Collection of railroad blueprints from the private collection of historian Henry Bender, Jr.

Research notes from an unpublished inventory of depots , Henry Bender, Jr.

Index

TILE RO
PASA
W. I.
6'-7"
2'-11"